Y0-BYF-748

Michael M. Klepper was a pioneer in the field of broadcast public relations. Formerly a network writer, producer, and director, he now heads Michael Klepper Associates, a public relations agency. He is also an adjunct professor at New York University.

I've spent years at some of the best public relations agencies, Carl Byoir and Burson Marsteller among them, where I've met some pretty good writers. None of them come close to Audrey Fisher.

I mention her because this book is as much Audrey's as it is mine. We wrote it together.

I dedicate it to her, my co-worker, my co-author, my friend.

Michael M. Klepper

GETTING YOUR MESSAGE OUT

How to Get, Use, and Survive
Radio & Television Air Time

A SPECTRUM BOOK

PRENTICE-HALL, INC.
Englewood Cliffs, New Jersey 07632

Library of Congress Cataloging in Publication Data

Klepper, Michael M.
  Getting your message out.

  "A Spectrum Book."
  Includes index.
  1. Public relations. 2. Publicity. 3. Radio in
publicity. 4. Television broadcasting. 5. Mass media
and business. I. Title.
HM263.K56 1984   659.2   83-26873
ISBN 0-13-354648-9
ISBN 0-13-354630-6 (pbk.)

A SPECTRUM BOOK

10 9 8 7 6 5 4 3 2 1

Printed in the United States of America

Editorial/production supervision by Cyndy Lyle Rymer
Manufacturing buyer: Joyce Levatino
Cover and jacket design by Hal Siegel

ISBN 0-13-354648-9

ISBN 0-13-354630-6

Prentice-Hall International, Inc., *London*
Prentice-Hall of Australia Pty Limited, *Sydney*
Prentice-Hall Canada Inc., *Toronto*
Prentice-Hall of India Private Limited, *New Delhi*
Prentice-Hall of Japan, Inc., *Tokyo*
Prentice-Hall of Southeast Asia Pte. Ltd., *Singapore*
Whitehall Books Limited, *Wellington, New Zealand*
Editora Prentice-Hall do Brasil Ltda., *Rio de Janeiro*

Contents

Preface

This book was written to help all those who want or need to tell their stories on radio and television intelligently, effectively, and often. Its advice is directed to the novice public relations practitioner who needs practical step-by-step suggestions, the professional who knows there's a better way of understanding and working with broadcasters but hasn't quite been able to put a finger on it, the entrepreneur with a small business who's been invited to talk about her company on a local talk show and wants to back out, the chief executive of a major corporation who's ashamed to admit how intimidating those television cameras are, even after all these years.

I've wanted to write this book for more than a decade, since I was a producer at NBC at the outset of the consumer and environmental movements of the 1960s. I thought then that people who represented business and nonprofit organizations to the broadcast media were badly in need of some friendly guidance on how to turn radio and television reporters from adversaries to allies. I still think so.

In the 1960s, knowing how to work with radio and television was an asset (and a rare one indeed) in the field of public relations. Today, it's absolutely crucial. The average American family spends more than a fourth of each and every twenty-four hour day watching television. We rely on radio and television as our first and most believeable sources of news and information. The broadcast media entertain, inform, amuse, challenge, soothe, and enlighten us probably more than any other single force in our lives.

Today there are new opportunities and challenges in the broadcast arena. Paralleling the growth in the power and reach of traditional broadcast media—radio and television—have been dramatic changes in the kinds of delivery systems available today in the average American home—or likely to be available tomorrow.

Cable television is an example. It lay virtually dormant throughout the 1960s and 1970s. Today, it has shed that sleeping tiger image and is grabbing an ever-increasing share of the broadcast audience and offering a new diversity of programming options to viewers.

Another example is satellite technology, as new to the electronic media as the launching of the first communications satellite, Satcom I, in 1975. Then, only a handful of giant communications monopolies could afford to build an earth station to pull in signals from the circling satellite. Today, your neighbor may very well have an inexpensive dish in the backyard, and rooftop earth stations may soon be bypassing traditional network programming and providing direct satellite access to households all over the world.

Interactive video, teletext, videotex, direct broadcast satellites, teleconferencing, video cassettes, shopping by satellite, computer banking, videodisks—some are significant new advances in the communications industry, some are electronic gadgets heralded today and forgotten tomorrow. But all are part of the fascinating and ever-changing new media mix created and thrust upon us by the technological revolution that is still unfolding today.

Being part of that whole exciting media mix is no longer optional for those in the public relations profession. It's imperative. If you want to communicate effectively with the American public, you must get your message where the audience is—and that audience is listening to the radio, watching TV, and experimenting with the new mass communication technologies.

Broadcast is a means of mass communication. So are newspapers and magazines. But there the resemblance ends. In these pages, I've tried to tell you why radio and television are different, how they're different, and most importantly, how you must be different in your approach to getting your story told effectively on their airwaves. The advice is practical, down-to-earth, easy to follow, and, as I've illustrated by dozens of case histories from my own experience and the experience of my closest colleagues, it works.

There is much speculation today about where the broadcast media are heading. The never-ending parade of technological innovations (here or on the horizon) promise to "make television as we know it today look like a relic in five years," in the words of futurist Alvin Toffler.

We can only guess where all these technological miracles are taking us. But we can be sure of this: The broadcast media may change in three years or five or ten . . . perhaps dramatically. But the techniques for working with broadcast—the techniques described in these pages—will still work as well for you then as they do today.

The delivery systems may change, but the message, the story, will always be the central concern of the audience. Business, industry, and nonprofit organizations have a story to tell. The public relations professionals are the storytellers.

Learn to tell your story on radio and television today, and you will be a part of the media mix for years to come.

Introduction

Public relations! The images still favored by too many producers of Hollywood films and television sit-coms—the flesh-pumping, omnipresent publicity hound or, worse yet, the typewriter-bound flack cranking out press releases in a dusty back room and cowering before the boss—are as outdated as the silent movie and black-and-white TV.

Those stereotypes of yesteryear have been supplanted by today's reality—the new public relations professional. This is the sophisticated vice president of corporate communications, with an office three doors down from the chief executive, an upper level income, a staff of five or fifteen or twenty-five, meaningful access to corporate policymakers, and most of all, enormous responsibilities that include monitoring attitudes of the public toward the company, and shaping the company's position and image and then reflecting them honestly and effectively to the public.

Public relations today is a respected profession. It's respected for its ability to increase public awareness of a product or service, enhance the image of a business enterprise or a charitable organization, boost sales, create excitement, lobby effectively for new legislation, help elect candidates to public office, increase donations, recruit volunteers, change public attitudes, and increase the value of a company's stock.

It's not only a handful of Fortune 500 companies that are recognizing the power and impact of public relations in the successful conduct of their daily affairs. In smaller businesses across the country, in entrepreneurial enterprises struggling for a foothold, in large and small charitable and nonprofit organizations, in municipal offices and school districts, universities and trade organizations, public relations professionals are being accorded new respect and ever greater opportunities, responsibilities, and challenges.

Public relations has grown tremendously over the past three decades. Paralleling that growth has been an even more visible and more astounding increase in another segment of the communications industry—the broadcast media: radio, television, and more recently, a mind boggling array of alternative delivery systems like cable television, direct broadcast satellites, teletext and videotex, and teleconferencing.

BROADCAST AS A PUBLIC RELATIONS VEHICLE

In the infant years of public relations (and of radio and television), broadcast was rarely considered a significant ingredient in the public relations recipe. Most public relations practitioners were alumni of the print media; they were former reporters at newspapers, wire services, magazines, or trade books. Thus, print generally dominated the field. The ultimate public relations goal was almost universally to arrange an interview with a key newspaper or wire service writer, or to succeed in having an article written about your product, service, or event. In those rare cases where an interview with the boss on television or radio was arranged, it was viewed as a pleasant extra, as icing on the cake, not to be taken seriously, but "nice." "Hey, that was real nice," the boss might say, "but now show me the clips!"

That, too, is finally changing, at least among the more savvy and sophisticated of the "new breed" of public relations professionals. Today, broadcast is (or should be) an integral part of every comprehensive public relations strategy. Some major corporations are so involved in broadcast that they have in-house television studios that would make many a commercial broadcaster turn green with envy. They are producing their own shows, both for internal and external consumption, with quality and production values that rival anything the commercial stations have to offer. Many are involved in satellite distribution, teleconferencing, the production of video news features of enough general interest to be broadcast via the public airwaves or cable systems around the country.

Most of us in the public relations field don't work for corporations who can devote that kind of talent and that level of bucks to broadcast public relations. But today, with radio and television more powerful than ever before, with myriad new technologies and challenges on the broadcast horizon, we too are learning how important it is to work comfortably, effectively, and regularly with the broadcast media.

But public relations people are not the only ones who need to recognize the importance of the electronic media to our companies and organizations. Just as critical to an effective, meaningful multimedia program are the attitudes and skills of decision makers of business and industry, the corporate officers and members of the board, the marketing managers and department heads, and the directors, key staffers, and volunteers of nonprofit organizations.

It is these executives who make policy and set the direction and the pace for their companies and organizations. They are the people who must decide, once and for all, to move the company's public relations department out of that dusty backroom and into the fast paced world of electronic communications. They are the individuals who, in almost every case, will be called upon to "meet the press" and "face the nation"—to overcome their apprehension, and to speak for their companies and organizations on radio and television.

Broadcast public relations! The innovative, the courageous, the leaders of business, industry, and volunteer organizations are doing it. In these pages, you'll learn why, and then you'll learn how. And soon you'll be doing it too, with results that will please and astound you.

BROADCAST PUBLIC RELATIONS
FOR EXECUTIVES AND PRACTITIONERS

This text is targeted to two audiences: the company or organization executive who creates the policy and establishes the parameters of responsibility for his or her employees, and the public relations professional who must develop the skills and techniques to help create the parameters and then carry them out.

All the information and suggestions presented here will prove valuable to any person with the desire to learn more about the values, the goals, and the techniques of broadcast public relations. However, there are some portions of the text that are specifically directed to the executive, and others that are addressed to the public relations professional. The following is a roadmap of the organization of the text.

The "Why" of Broadcast Public Relations

The book opens with a two chapter overview that should be read by both the executive and the practitioner. Chapter One describes in some detail the critical differences between the traditional print media with which we're all so familiar and the broadcast media—radio, television and newer forms of electronic communications. (The topic may sound elementary, but as you'll see, there are profound differences between the media—differences which dramtically impact on how the broadcast media is approached.) For those who still hesitate and who aren't sure whether or how broadcast public relations will help their company or organization, Chapter Two describes the smorgasbord of opportunities available to your company or organization in radio, television and the new technologies.

These two chapters make up the "why" of broadcast public

relations. I challenge you to read them and then dare to say "Radio is not for us," or "I just don't think we're ready yet for TV."

The "How" for the Public Relations Professional

Chapters Three through Eight also contain materials of value to both the executive and the public relations practitioner. The executive may want to review them to get a feel for the kind of skills and expertise needed by public relations people in order to work effectively with radio, television, and the new technologies.

But the materials demand a closer reading by those men and women who will be dealing with broadcasters on a day-to-day basis; the public relations professionals at companies or organizations across America. In this section, you'll find a step-by-step, how-to guide covering every aspect of broadcast public relations. We'll show you how to make those first contacts with the broadcast decision makers in your company and at national radio, television, and cable networks. We'll describe how to build meaningful professional relationships with broadcasters based on your awareness of their unique needs. We'll tell you how to write a news release that is tailored for broadcast, and how to phrase a query letter to make it irresistible to the recipient at your radio or television station.

Next, we'll delve into the real fun and the real challenges of broadcast public relations. In Chapter Six, you'll learn how to format your story to make it work on radio or television. You'll learn to think like a producer, to help your story attain the attention it deserves. In Chapter Seven, you'll find a step-by-step how-to guide to one of the mainstays of broadcast public relations—the media tour. You'll learn to take your story on the road, and to plan a media tour that would be the envy of any Madison Avenue agency. And finally, in Chapter Eight, you'll learn the rudiments of producing your own broadcast materials for radio, for television, and for the new delivery systems.

The "How" for the Executive

It's essential that someone in your organization know how to approach the electronic media and work effectively with broadcast reporters to communicate the message of your company or organization.

But in these days of powerful consumerism, freedom of information, increased public interest in business and industry, and the rapidly multiplying number of broadcast programs focusing on news and information, odds are that some day, probably very soon, the broadcast media will be approaching *you.* The microphones will be pointed in your direction, the cameras will be in your office and you'll find yourself on the evening news whether or not you want to be there.

Therefore, the final two chapters are directed primarily at the company or organization executive—the individual who will be carrying the flag, who must face the interviewer on radio or television, and who needs to react decisively and effectively in the face of a crisis that has the potential for damaging public opinion. In nearly every instance that person is not a spokesperson from the public relations department, but is the "top dog," the key decision-maker, the man or woman who knows the story best.

All too often, executives who agree in theory that the electronic media are important change their tune when faced with the prospect of a live interview on radio or under the studio lights. That's just not realistic today. And it's not necessary. Just as the skills and techniques for working with broadcasters can be mastered by any dedicated person, so can any savvy executive master the attitudes and techniques that will lead to effective, believable radio and television interviews. These attitudes and techniques are the topics of Chapter Nine.

In the final chapter, we'll discuss how to be sure you're considering the special needs of the broadcast reporter when your company or organization is involved in a crisis situation.

In short, this book is a how-to course in broadcast public relations, both for the public relations professional and the company or organization executive. It covers all the techniques and skills you need to tell your story and to communicate your message on radio or television.

The broadcast media are in a constant state of growth, development, and change. It is not easy to predict what they will be like tomorrow. No matter what exciting innovations appear in the communications arena, however, we can be sure of one constant. Radio and television are, and always will be, the most intimate and direct of media. They are, and always will be, one person talking to another. Whether you're a recent journalism school graduate looking for your first job or a seasoned public relations professional, whether you've just formed your own company or are the marketing manager at a billion-dollar corporation, you need to understand what the electronic media are all about.

And that's what this book is all about.

part one

THE
WHY
OF BROADCAST
PUBLIC RELATIONS

chapter one

Radio and Television: An Overview

Radio and television are different from print.

At first glance, that is not a very provocative statement. But it is the premise of this book and when you truly understand it, you'll hold the key to a whole new approach to public relations and a whole new way of communicating with the public.

Franklin Delano Roosevelt understood the difference in 1933, the year he broadcast on radio the first of his famous "Fireside Chats." Desperate people across the nation propped their President's photo atop their radios and gathered, in the intimacy of their own living rooms, to listen to and be cheered by his assurances of a coming prosperity. That year, before Roosevelt's first radio chat on March 12, one federal employee handled all the presidential mail. In the last two weeks of March, a half million letters deluged the White House, according to historian Arthur Schlesinger. Schlesinger called Roosevelt's radio talks "a milestone in politics and broadcasting." [1]

Writer Rod Serling understood the difference in 1955, when his original television drama, "Passages," aired on the popular "Kraft TV Theater." The struggling unknown became an instant celebrity; within two weeks, he received 23 offers of TV assignments, three movie offers and 14 requests for newspaper and magazine interviews.[2]

Lyndon Johnson, just installed as President after the

3

brutal assassination of his predecessor, experienced the difference. "On that unforgettable weekend in November, 1963, television provided a personal experience which all could share, a vast religious service which all could attend, a unifying bond which all could feel," [3] Mr. Johnson recalled. Radio and television audiences have shared many other such unifying experiences in the past four decades, from the terror of Orson Welles' "War of the Worlds" radio broadcast in 1938 to the televised Watergate hearings of the 1970s.

Neil Armstrong understood it in 1969, when an estimated 723 million people from 47 countries, more than a fifth of the world's population, watched television in awe as he took that "one small step for a man, one giant leap for mankind." [4]

Today, the power and influence of the broadcast media are not debatable. Radio and television are the acknowledged center ring, the main arena for the distribution of news and information, the "central nervous system of America," in the words of one expert observer. It's through the broadcast media that the majority of Americans receive news and information. For many Americans, they are the exclusive source of news.

Despite their acknowledged influence, radio and television too often remain the neglected stepchildren for public relations specialists in many otherwise savvy business and non-profit institutions. A surprisingly large number of these professionals, and the company and organization executives they represent, still think of the printed word, newspapers, and magazines as the primary outlet for their stories and messages. Radio and television are considered secondary vehicles, if they're considered at all. Perhaps it is fear or distrust of the unknown. Perhaps it is the difficulty of assessing results. (There's no scrapbook of clippings to send to the executive suite.) Perhaps it is the transitory character of the electronic media. Perhaps it is inexperience, or skepticism, or lack of insight.

Whatever the reason, the failure to make radio and television an integral part of your public relations strategy can be shortsighted. If you want to communicate effectively with the American public, you need to get your message to the audience.

Following are some specific characteristics of broadcast that distinguish it from print as a medium for news and information.

IMMEDIACY

A newspaper or magazine reader learns of an event after the fact. He or she reads a synthesized version of the event, is told how someone else (the reporter) heard, saw and experienced it. Even the best news writing is secondhand, third person, past tense.

The radio listener or television viewer doesn't receive a secondhand, synthesized account. He or she sees and hears each story as it unfolds. The audience is propelled into the situation, and almost becomes a part of the action; in Cape Canaveral, thrilling to the explosive ascent of a sleek spaceship; in Washington, viewing the horror of yet another attempt on the life of a political leader; in Beirut or Poland or northern Ireland, witnessing the travesties and tragedies of war and violence; in the concert halls of the Met or the Philharmonic.

The very names of your local newscasts convey that sense of immediacy: "Action News," "Live at Five," "Newsmaker," "Eyewitness News." Through broadcast, in the words of that pioneer radio journalist Edward R. Murrow, "You are there." For the sports fan, it's eminently more satisfying to see the Superbowl on television than to read about it the next day in the morning newspaper. For a gourmet cook, there's an immense difference between reading a recipe in *Good Housekeeping* and watching Julia Child concoct it in a studio kitchen.

Broadcast's immediacy makes it very attractive to the savvy public relations professional. In broadcast, you bring your story or message directly to the listener or viewer. There's no intermediator, and no extra layer of synthesis.

TRANSIENCE

Radio and television deal with fleeting images. The story or message is there and then it's gone. You can't retrieve it unless you take the trouble to tape it on your VCR and replay it. You can't go back and reread it as you would a newspaper story or magazine article. You can't pause and reflect on what you've just seen or heard unless you turn off the set or mentally close out the next images confronting you.

Broadcast's transience means many listeners and viewers may not comprehend or retain much of what they see and hear on radio or television. A researcher at Purdue University recently found that more than 90 percent of 2,700 people tested misunderstood even such straightforward fare as televised commercials or a popular detective sitcom. Only minutes after watching, the typical viewer in that study missed 23 to 36 percent of questions about what had been broadcast.[5]

The lesson here for the public relations professional is clear. In broadcast situations you need to work very hard to clarify, simplify, and distill your story or message. If you don't, the audience won't remember it, or worse, may never comprehend it at all.

IMPACT

Who among those who saw it will ever forget the television portrait of the young girl in South Vietnam, running naked and aflame down a highway with the sounds of war roaring behind her? That single picture may have taught more Americans more about the realities of war than all the printed analyses ever published.

Broadcast is a natural story teller. Television, especially, deals in drama, in situations, and in action. Its stories are alive. Its impressions are vivid and often lasting. It awakens and assaults the senses with visual and audio sensations.

In television, with its compressed time frame, pictures are often used to replace words. News reports and feature scripts are mostly written around the available pictures. Many critics believe that television's emphasis on drama and its reliance on visuals have a tendency to distort reality. To the extent that this is true, it is a major limitation of the medium.

There is another noteworthy consequence of television's dependence on visuals. Because broadcasters are so concerned about visual impact, some may tend to overlook or ignore some significant information or important ideas because they are difficult to portray dramatically or visually. Until very recently, business and financial news was nearly totally absent from television, largely because these stories, though admittedly important, didn't "have good visuals." Today, of course, that's changing. More Americans demand solid news coverage of economics and finance. In response to that, broadcasters have found more creative ways to portray economic stories visually; with charts and graphs, background footage, on-location shots, animation, logos and computer graphics.

When you have a story to tell or information to transmit on television, you need to consider how it can be portrayed dramatically through visuals.

INTIMACY

In broadcast, the news and information of the day is brought to you by familiar voices and faces. If you were to invite James Reston, the *New York Times* columnist, to your next cocktail party, chances are most of your friends wouldn't recognize him until he introduced himself. But if Walter Cronkite, Barbara Walters, or Tom Brokaw stopped in at your party, probably almost everyone would turn and say, "My God, isn't that Walter . . . Barbara . . . Tom?"

Broadcast is a very personal, very intimate form of news and information delivery. There is Peter Jennings, Roger Mudd, or Dan Rather, sitting in your family room, telling you all about what happened that day. And because they're so familiar, and their delivery of news and information is so intimate and personal, the typical broadcast journalist inspires a certain degree of trust in the mind of the viewer or listener.

Inevitably, this intimate form of news and information delivery permits some degree of subtle editorialization in its broadcast reports. Doubtless much of it is inadvertent, accidental. But the fact remains that a smile, frown, or lift of the eyebrow as your favorite anchorperson leads into a story, reacts to one, or introduces a guest can become more than a casual gesture. That fleeting facial expression, that body English, that nuance, transmits a subtle opinion, endorsing the message or condemning it.

When you recognize the advantages, and the potential dangers, of broadcast's personalized, intimate style, you will be better able to predict which ideas and interviews will "work" on radio and television, and which won't.

CAPSULIZED

Radio and television are often called "headline services." Someone once remarked that the entire content of the eleven o'clock news would comprise just one column in *The New York Times*. Whether or not that's true, even the most casual observer knows that broadcast segments, for the most part, are very brief and capsulized. The average radio news story is under thirty seconds. Most television news segments average sixty to ninety seconds. An "in-depth" broadcast interview usually doesn't go over five to seven minutes.

Some broadcast innovators are introducing news and information programs with less condensed, abbreviated, distilled formats. Consider, for example, the trend to more and longer newscasts; in-depth public affairs reporting by skilled broadcast journalists like Robert MacNeil, James Lehrer, Bill Moyers, and Ted Koppel, as well as the advent of twenty-four hour news and talk programming, first in radio, then in television. Many of these efforts are scoring high with critics and audiences alike. It appears the public's thirst for news and information still hasn't been satisfied.

For the most part, radio and television are still prisoners of time. The hour has only sixty minutes. It can be divided but not expanded. And broadcast time is valuable. Minutes, even fractions of minutes, can be sold for thousands of dollars on the ad-supported broadcast networks and stations. That, in itself, is a strong motivation to compress and abbreviate.

In their pursuit of high ratings, broadcasters must also bow to commercial demands for programming that attracts and holds the attention of the viewer or listener. That, at least according to current wisdom, means fast paced programming with shorter and more varied segments. In his *The Right Place at the Right Time,* Robert MacNeil, a broadcast journalist who has made some successful efforts to buck that trend says, "We knew television viewers were conditioned to expect pace, action, visual variety, tension and minimal demands on their attention span." [6] Indeed, research shows attention spans are getting shorter and shorter, perhaps partially because of exposure to broadcast media.

A leisurely paced interview, an in-depth analysis of your product or service, may be appropriate when you're working with a reporter from your local newspaper or the trade magazine that covers your field. But in dealing with the broadcast media, you are subject to severe time limitations, just as radio and television journalists are. You need to understand that and plan your presentation accordingly.

SIMPLICITY

Time constraints can sometimes lead to inaccuracies and distortions in broadcast coverage of news and information. Veteran television journalist Av Westin explains in his fascinating book, *Newswatch,* "Because programs have to begin when they are scheduled, editorial decisions are affected. The evening newscasts often go on the air with less than complete information. A newspaper can delay printing its editions by several minutes while waiting for more details on a story. Television cannot delay for even one second, and once something is eliminated or missed on a broadcast, it is gone forever." [7]

Broadcasters work hard to overcome or deal more creatively with time constraints. But those limitations and the resulting superficialities still remain. When a newspaper or magazine does a comprehensive round-up story on a current issue, the reporter will probably interview and quote dozens of sources expressing a wide variety of viewpoints. When radio or television covers the same topic, even though many resources may be interviewed and investigated, chances are only two or three will get on air to express a view or offer an insight. The usual result is a "balanced" presentation offering views that are black and white—one from the right, one from the left, and the correspondent concluding the segment with the comment that "the truth probably lies somewhere in the middle."

ACCESSIBILITY

You don't have to walk down to the corner news stand to buy them or wait for your neighbor's son or daughter to deliver them to your door. Radio and television are accessible to you twenty-four hours a day. You just flip the dial, flick the switch, sit back and they come to you, practically wherever you are.

Today, more than 99 percent of American homes and 96 percent of American cars are equipped with radios.[8] We take them with us wherever we go; to the beach, to the shopping center, on the way to or from the office. We listen to our radios while we're busy doing other things, such as pressing tablecloths, driving, raking leaves, sunning ourselves at the backyard pool, and even (if we're to believe our teenaged offspring), doing homework!

Today, more people get their first news of the morning by radio than by any other medium; radio reaches over 96 percent of Americans every week, more than any other communications medium, according to statistics of the Radio Advertising Bureau.

Television's reach and influence today is even greater. More than 98 percent of American homes are equipped with television sets; over 50 percent have two or more sets. Daily hours of viewing in the average American home continue their upward climb: five hours, nine minutes in 1961; six hours, one minute in 1971; six hours, forty-four minutes in 1981.[9]

In a recent Roper poll, two-thirds of the Americans questioned cited television as their major source of news and information.

REGULATION BY GOVERNMENT

America's broadcast industry is unique in that it's probably the only industry that ever came to the federal government petitioning for regulation. Industry pleas for regulation came in the 1920s, when more individuals and groups than could be accommodated on available frequencies were applying for licenses to broadcast.

The resulting chaos was resolved by the Radio Act of 1927, forerunner of the Communications Act of 1934. The federal legislation created the Federal Communications Commission, a seven-member body appointed by Congress to regulate broadcast stations in the "public interest, convenience and necessity."

FCC regulations must pass First Amendment standards; the 1934 Communications Act specifically forbids censorship of programming by the regulatory agency. Yet the FCC's power to approve and renew broadcast licenses provides a powerful tool for influencing the content of programming. Regulations cover a wide range of broadcast activities. A complete summary of FCC rules and regulations is found in *Broadcasting Year-book* (see Chapter Three).

Today the power of government to regulate radio and television stations is the subject of increasing question and debate. Many argue that broadcasters should have the same freedom from government interference enjoyed by the American press under the First Amendment. Others believe that government regulations, though once necessary, are outmoded today.

More and more influential Americans are climbing onto the deregulation bandwagon as new technologies erode the once clear difference between television and print and challenge the "scarcity of airwaves" concept that was the initial impetus for government regulation of broadcast.

The extent to which government should control communications in a nation with a strong free press tradition is certain to be a major issue of debate in the months and years ahead. Ultimately, it seems clear that there will be dramatic changes made in the regulatory atmosphere of the broadcast industry.

The Fairness Doctrine

Of all broadcast regulations, the one of most interest to public relations professionals is the much discussed Fairness Doctrine, adopted by the FCC in 1959 in an attempt to assure equitable broadcast treatment of "controversial issues of public interest and importance." Under this doctrine, the broadcast licensee is obliged to "afford reasonable opportunities for the discussion of conflicting views on issues of public importance."

Under the Fairness Doctrine, broadcasters have an obligation to deal with issues they deem of public importance; they must not present just one viewpoint on the issues they cover. The doctrine does, however, allow broadcasters much discretion in how their obligations to "fairness" will be met and which issues will be aired. Each station can choose which of many contrasting views will be presented and what persons will present those views. Consequently, no individual or group can claim the right to state its side of an issue as a condition of the Fairness Doctrine. The broadcaster determines how and when the issue will be presented.

In other words, the Fairness Doctrine does not confer a right of access to the airwaves to any person or group. The only right of access is for ideas, and for the public debate of issues deemed to be of public interest. Broadcasters can fulfill their fairness obligations without permitting anyone outside the station to use their broadcast facilities.

The Personal Attack Rule

The Personal Attack Rule, adopted by the FCC in 1967, makes the Fairness Doctrine more concrete, allowing the broadcaster less discretion in instances where a person or group has been attacked on air. The rule requires that when an identifiable person or group is attacked on radio or television, the licensee must notify the attacked party, provide a script, tape, or summary of the attack and offer a reasonable opportunity to respond. The rule applies to corporations and organizations, but not to foreigners or political candidates or to attacks made during a "news or news-type" program.

This regulation, unlike the Fairness Doctrine, does guarantee access to the airwaves under specified conditions.

The Equal Time Rule

Of less importance to public relations professionals, except for those who are working for a political candidate, is the Equal Time Rule, part of federal regulation since 1927. This regulation requires licensees to provide "equal time" for all declared candidates for a public office, provided the broadcaster initiates the requirement by allowing another declared candidate for the same office to use or purchase airtime. News and news-type programs are exempt from the equal time rule.

TECHNOLOGICAL EXPLOSION

Cable television, MDS, STV, pay-per-view. Satellites, earth stations, unscramblers and decoders, Teletext, videotex, DBS, Qube.

We are literally in the midst of a technological revolution in the electronic communications industry. The electronic media are changing so fast that what one says or writes about them today may well be outdated tomorrow.

With that caution in mind, following is a brief overview of the new technologies and new delivery systems, here and on the horizon.

Advent of the Satellite

The launch of Satcom I by RCA in 1975 may well have been the most far-reaching breakthrough in the communications field since the invention of the telegraph more than 140 years earlier.

The launch of the first commercial satellite fired a technological explosion in the electronic media, offering new listening and viewing diversity to the public and new opportunites for profit to the aggressive entrepreneur.

Today, an increasing number of orbiting space vehicles hover 22,300 miles above the equator, relaying signals around the world in split seconds, linking city to city and nation to nation in an instantaneous, intimate global communications network.

Satellites distribute programming to commercial networks and their affiliates, to public broadcast and independent stations. Through satellites, powerful new networks are made possible, and small cable systems are interconnected, offering them the rich diversity of programming demanded by increasingly discriminating viewers. Independent production companies, large or small, can rent satellite space and create instant syndicates, making their materials available to local stations and local systems from coast to coast. Satellite-fed press conferences, satellite shopping, speakers offered via satellite—all are communications options that were the stuff of dreams just a decade ago.

Cable Television

Cable television, the technology of distributing television signals to homes by wire rather than over the air, has been on the scene since before 1950. But until the advent of the satellite, cable was seen primarily as a means to bring telecasts to isolated areas not served by over-the-air signals. As an industry or a viable communications medium, cable had attracted little attention.

All that has changed. Spurred by new technological advances and by a gradual program of deregulation undertaken by the FCC during the 1970s, cable television has expanded rapidly. By the end of 1982, more than a third of American homes were linked to cable systems, doubling the reach of just three years earlier; experts were predicting a 50 to 60 percent reach by the end of the decade. Although many older cable systems were still limited to as few as twelve channels, by 1982, new systems were being installed across the country with as many as 120 channels available.

To fill those many channels, an unprecedented range and diversity of programming, much of it directed to specific, focused audiences, is making its presence felt in the communications industy. Advertiser-supported networks vie with pay channels financed by monthly payments from viewers for the attention and loyalty of increasingly diffused and scattered audiences. There are networks directed just to children, to Spanish-speaking viewers, to sports lovers, and to those interested in health or news, public affairs or business.

As more Americans become linked to cable systems with unprecedented numbers of channels, there will be opportunities for even more diversity, even more "narrowcasting." Special channels may be devoted to increasingly specific audiences—bridge players, stamp collectors, railroad buffs, antique dealers, jazz musicians—much as the magazine industry of today has evolved. Whether sufficient audiences and/or revenues can be found to support those many options is still a subject of debate. As one network newscaster asks with some skepticism: "All that programming—for whom?"

Interactive Cable Systems

Initiated by the Warner-Amex Qube experiment installed in Columbus, Ohio in the late 1970s, interactive cable systems allow viewers to "talk back" to their television sets, thus extending dramatically the smorgasbord of programming and service options available through cable.

Shop-at-home and bank-at-home services, information retrieval, and two-way burglary and fire protection are just some services provided via interactive cable. Customers with "addressable boxes" linked to their sets can receive "pay-per-view" programming, allowing the cable company to release special programming and bill just those households whose sets were tuned to receive it.

Over-the-Air Technologies

Installing a cable system, particularly in a major metropolitan area, is a costly and time consuming process. For that reason, a variety of over-the-air alternatives to cable franchises have developed, each threatening to draw potential cable subscribers in the increasingly competitive media marketplace.

STV, subscription television, was the first over-the-air alternative to cable. It distributes programming via a conventional television channel by sending a scrambled signal; a decoder in a box attached to the viewer's television set unscrambles the signal. Viewers pay a monthly rental fee for the decoder.

Multipoint distribution services (MDS) uses microwaves to beam programming over the air to a rooftop antenna. Because of low installation costs and the speed of installation, it has proven a popular alternative where feasible. MDS is limited in use, however, since it requires a clear "line of sight" from the transmission point to the antenna; foliage or taller surrounding buildings impede that line of sight and thus make transmission impossible.

SMATV, satellite master antenna television, does not have the physical limitations of MDS, and thus has been widely used to provide cable programming to occupants of large multiple-unit dwellings, where costs of installation can be absorbed by a number of households. SMATV buildings are equipped with a rooftop dish which receives satellite-delivered programming; the programming is then delivered by wire to receiving apartments. Theoretically, SMATV can deliver as many channels as a cable system.

The most discussed and potentially most revolutionary over-the-air delivery system, however, is DBS, direct broadcast satellite, which many have called "television's next frontier." By the end of 1982, the FCC had approved nine applications for DBS services, despite the objections of the networks.

DBS systems will beam a collection of original programming channels directly to homes equipped with inexpensive dish receivers, bypassing the conventional television programming distributors, notably the major networks. It promises more diversity and more programming choices to areas already served by cable systems; additionally, it will offer first-time service to areas not yet linked to cable or over-the-air systems.

Information Services

Pioneered in Great Britain and widely used in other European countries, the concept of an "electronic newspaper" has sparked great interest and several experimental programs in the communications industry.

Teletext, a one-way system, allows television stations to transmit, invisibly and during regular broadcast hours, several hundred "pages" of information to the viewer's television set in printed form. An index lists the information available that day. Each page is numbered, so the viewer can punch up the information desired and hold it on the screen as long as he or she wishes.

A potential alternative or supplement to the print media, teletext can list the day's headlines with page numbers showing where more detail is available. Advertisers can use teletex to provide detailed local information supplementing national ads. Viewers can receive recipes, television and movie schedules, marketing tips, airline and train schedules (with up-to-the-minute changes and delays), current stock market reports, and a wide variety of other services.

Videotex is an interactive information service providing the viewer with two-way access to that same smorgasbord of information. The difference is the viewer can then act on that information—order products, reserve theater tickets, or make travel reservations through a computer terminal linked to the household television set.

In Summary

All these technological innovations, new programming and distribution options are the focus of much discussion in the communications industry today. Which will thrive? Which will fail?

The future of the electronic media is still unfolding. As public relations professionals, we can play an active role in this exciting and challenging industry, no matter what direction it takes. We need to keep informed, to know about the new technologies and the new opportunities as they unfold. But more important is to remember our own critical role, that of sharing a message with the radio and television audiences of America.

The delivery systems may change. But the message, the story, will always be the central concern of the audience. In our role as the storytellers, we will be part of the media mix for many years to come.

chapter two

Identifying Broadcast Opportunities

Your local rock and roll radio station announces it is turning to an all-talk format. A local television newscast expands from ninety minutes to two hours, and a competing station responds by expanding its evening news from two hours to three. Your city gets linked to cable, and you suddenly find you have thirty, fifty, or even one hundred new channels to choose from. Networks have all-night newscasts, or if you are a cable subscriber, you can flip your dial to news and information twenty-four hours a day, not just from one source, but several.

Opportunities! There are more for you every day in the fast-moving, ever-changing fields of radio and television.

A half century ago, federal lawmakers cited scarcity of air time as a major reason why broadcasters should be subjected to fairness rules and other regulations far more stringent than those imposed on print journalism. Today, it is newspapers that are in short supply. The city or town served by more than one daily newspaper is rare. Even when there are two dailies, more often than not they are both owned by the same company.

In contrast, the number of competing radio and television stations (over 10,000 today) has expanded beyond the wildest dreams of the regulators of the Hoover and Roosevelt generations. In major metropolitan areas or tiny mountainous hamlets, most Americans can choose from numerous AM and FM radio stations. Nearly everyone can tune into three or more television stations. In increasing numbers, American homes are linked to cable systems which dramatically expand broadcast choices, or they are equipped with technological devices designed to create more access to news, information, and entertainment.

Wherever you live and work, there has been an explosion of opportunities for you in the broadcast media. And it's still widening. Here is a quick survey of the many local and national resources available to help you tell your company or organization's story on radio or television:

LOCAL RADIO OPPORTUNITIES

In the early heyday of radio, networks dominated the airwaves and dictated programming. They created and perfected the entertainment formats still familiar today—the soap opera, the variety show, the situation comedy. They were the prime sources of news and information for growing audiences of eager listeners.

Today, radio is radically different. In growing numbers, networks still provide affiliates with national news, information, and feature material. But radio has become primarily a local medium. Its emphasis is on community service, community news and information, and community issues and concerns. While the networks battle with new technological delivery systems for a share of time on the tube, local radio continues to reach more people on a daily basis than any other information medium. To millions of Americans, the radio is like an old friend, turned on for an hour or two every day for music, news, information, or just out of habit.

Over 9,000 strong—and still growing in numbers, sophistication, and audience loyalty—radio stations are filling the airwaves with locally produced news, interviews, debates, and discussions. That means *opportunity* for your company or organization to communicate, often and effectively, with the people you most want to talk to—the people of your own home town.

Whether a station specializes in music or talk, whether it's AM or FM, network affiliated or independent, owned by private investors, a municipality or a university; whether it reaches listeners in a five-mile radius or a 150-mile radius, you can be sure it will offer plentiful opportunities for the news and information provided by your company or organization.

Here are some of the avenues you can explore to get into the local radio mix:

Radio News

Every radio station offers its listeners news. The amount and substance varies. Just about every good-sized city today has at least one local station with an all-news or expanded news/talk format. Journalists at these stations are aggressively looking for good local news and feature stories to inform, enlighten, and entertain their audiences. They are very likely to welcome your news releases and interview ideas, provided you set and maintain high standards of credibility and news judgement.

At the other end of the spectrum are contemporary, pop, or rock and roll music stations. Here, news may be limited to occasional five-minute reports with hourly thirty-second updates. But even those stations have news departments, and those news departments, no matter how small, report local news. Don't write them out of your script.

Between those two extremes are the vast majority of local radio stations dedicated to serving the community and its people. These stations air five- or ten-minute local newscasts every hour, or every half hour, and then supplement those newscasts with news updates throughout their regular programming.

Get to know the local news teams on the stations in your community (see Chapter Three for how-to) and make sure the news of your company or organization is incorporated into local radio newscasts.

Talk Shows

Not every radio station airs talk shows. But many do, and some make talk shows their specialty. Stations specializing in talk formats are probably not the most widely heard stations in their market areas, but they are generally in second or third place. More importantly, they command a loyal following.

Such an upscale audience is interested in ideas rather than wall-to-wall music. In short, it is *your* kind of audience.

Increasingly, radio talk shows specialize—in consumer topics, business, sports, education, religion, health and science, fitness, or fashion. Name a topic and there probably is a talk show somewhere discussing that topic every week.

The format of radio talk shows may vary—an interview by a newscaster or personality at the station, a debate with two or more guests discussing varying viewpoints on current issues, or a call-in program in which a guest expert fields phone calls, questions and comments from listeners.

Whatever its format, the talk show offers opportunity for people from your company or organization to participate as experts and perhaps to talk about the trends of your industry or field in general, your products or programs, the impact your company or organization has on the community, or your plans for the future.

Feature Segments

Whether or not they schedule regular talk shows, most stations do incorporate occasional brief news, information and feature items into their regular daily programming. These may be short feature reports or portions of a lengthy interview, edited into thirty-second or sixty-second "bites" and aired at key time periods throughout the broadcast day. One popular spot for these short segments is on morning or evening "drive time," the periods from 6 to 9 A.M. and 4 to 7 P.M. when most car and home radios are tuned in. Drive time programming offers a listening menu of music, news, sports, traffic, weather, and, perhaps, a phone interview with your company president or a feature story about your new fund-raising campaign.

Public Service Programming

Although radio stations are no longer required by the FCC to set aside a specified amount of air time for public service programming, many still do. Often, this programming takes the form of thirty-minute public affairs shows, heavily weighted toward local news and feature material. These programs can provide an effective forum for in-depth coverage of your company or organization and how it is serving the local community. Or, if you're involved in a controversial issue, the public service program may offer an effective platform for presenting your point of view.

Public service programs are rarely scheduled in prime listening time; more often than not, they are heard at "off-hours," on Saturday morning or late Sunday night. But any time someone puts a microphone in front of you and sends your words over the airwaves of America, you can be sure someone is out there hearing your message.

Editorials and Commentaries

Most radio stations air local editorials, offering the opinion of station management on matters of local concern. If a local editorial affects your company or organization, you have the right, and most stations encourage you, to ask for air time to respond. This can be a valuable opportunity to enhance your image or increase your visibility in the community.

Too often overlooked is the possibility of initiating radio editorials noting the positive impact your company or organization has on the community. Pick an appropriate time (you're expanding your plant, you've made a large donation to the local schools, you are sponsoring a major cultural event) and suggest it. You may be pleasantly surprised at the result.

PSAs and Community Calendars

Nearly all radio stations air PSAs (public service announcements), brief messages which inform the public of services available from your organization or request public support for your good works. PSAs are intended primarily to offer access to the airwaves to nonprofit organizations like the Cancer Society, United Way, Girl and Boy Scouts. This is not free air time for commercial ventures. If you represent a nonprofit group or if you want to communicate a message of genuine public importance, take advantage of the opportunity by providing stations with frequently updated, professionally prepared public service announcements.

For profit making organizations, many stations offer the opportunity to notify the public of special events or make short announcements of interest to the public via "Community Calendars." Use these forums when your company plans an open house or is sponsoring a seminar, an exhibition, or some other community program.

LOCAL TELEVISION OPPORTUNITIES

There is more competition and more diversity in local television today than ever before. Independently owned stations, public television, cable and other rapidly developing delivery systems are challenging the dominance of networks nationally, and of network affiliates in local markets. As these competitiors make inroads into the traditional audience share of the networks, local affiliates are beginning to flex their muscles and demand autonomy from the programming directives of the networks. They are asking, and getting, more opportunity to produce shows with a local identity to fend off the challenge of local competitors.

Improved technology is also contributing to the new autonomy and flexibility of local television stations. The satellite, once an exclusive toy of the networks, is now accessible to local stations, greatly increasing their programming options and lessening their dependence on network newsrooms. Some examples:

- A midwest station interviewed the parents of a local youth who who was one of America's hostages in Iran. The parents were in Europe; the interview was transmitted via satellite and aired live.
- A local newscast in Detroit included a broadcast beamed from

Tokyo. Viewers of the local news in Philadelphia saw scenes filmed that same day in Tehran.

- When the nation's Democrats met in New York to nominate a presidential candidate, viewers all over America had localized coverage of interviews with their own state's representatives, via satellite transmission.
- Major corporations and organizations now use the satellite to expand coverage of their news conferences by offering live link-up, via satellite, to the newsrooms of all cities where they have branches, customers, or clients.

The growing competition and the resultant emphasis on localized programming provides vast new opportunities for your company or organization to get a share of the air time available on local television.

Television News

Local television news, once considered a necessary evil and a sure dollar drain on stations, is thriving on local television stations across the country. No longer limited to an obligatory half-hour, local evening television broadcasts today range from one hour up to two or even three in some markets. Local news broadcasters aren't confined today to the pre-prime time hours; in most markets, they are seen throughout the day from early morning to late evening. Because viewership is up and ad revenues are strong, news has become a big money-maker.

Moreover, as local television expands the hours of its news coverage, local broadcasters are also expanding their definition of news. They are no longer content to limit their reports to the major events of the day such as fires, homicides, political rhetoric, and legislative decisions in the community. Instead local newscasts are supplementing that "hard news" with increasing doses of information and feature material: "All the things broadcasters believe viewers *want* to know about, as opposed to what they *ought* to know about," explains one local television newswoman. Or "news you can use," adds another.

This new emphasis on more balance, more so-called

"back of the book" news reporting, has meant a proliferation of feature-oriented correspondents on the local television news teams of America. Do not be surprised to learn your local station has a science editor, a business reporter, a consumer correspondent, and/or specialists in education, religion, arts and personal finance who are actively pursuing lively, informative, and timely feature ideas.

Talk Shows

Local versions of popular network morning shows like "Today" and "Good Morning, America" are produced in many local television studios of America. They are a fertile market for those "back of the book" feature ideas—interviews with interesting personnel from your company, and creative segments informing viewers about your unique new product or service.

A version of the talk show becoming increasingly popular on local television is the half-hour "magazine" format, featuring two or three stories of local interest, usually shot on location rather than in-studio. Frequently, they profile unusual people and original ideas. Sometimes these locally produced magazines are joined together in a loose network with similar programs in other communities; thus, a segment filmed in Toledo might be picked up by stations in Pittsburgh and Milwaukee and other cities across the country.

Independent stations and local cable channels are even more likely than the network affiliates to schedule frequent and provocative interview/discussion shows focusing on matters of local interest. Increasingly, television talk shows attempt to target a specific market—senior citizens, for example, or minorities or nonworking women, by focusing on topics of concern to those specific groups.

Public Service Programming

Many local television stations, both network affiliates and independents, provide public service programming as part of their efforts to meet licensing requirements to serve "the public interest, convenience and necessity." (See Chapter One.) As in local radio, you cannot expect these opportunities to be made available in prime time. However, regardless of when it airs, a public service program can be a very effective format for a half-hour documentary or a special report focusing on the contributions your company or organization or industry is making to the community.

Public service programming is becoming more and more original, aggressive, and professional. No longer content to focus on in-studio "talking-heads," producers are sending cameras on-location and using innovative, state-of-the-art graphics.

The burgeoning cable industry is providing many new opportunities for programming of a public service nature. All but the very smallest systems are required by FCC regulations to provide up to four access channels, to be made available for locally produced programming on a nondiscriminatory, first-come, first-served basis. Most cable systems today offer at least one such channel and originate a wide variety of programming in their own studios to meet that FCC requirement.

You can seek out local cable programming opportunities in two types of access channels. On public channels, programming opportunities are provided free of charge, though there may be a modest fee for use of the system's equipment, personnel, or production facilities. No overt commercial messages are allowed on public access channels. On lease channels, the cable system charges a fee for distributing your programming. Commercial messages are permitted.

Editorials and PSAs

Like local radio, the television stations of your community generally air the editorial opinions of station management on subjects of local concern. Like local radio, they are required to provide air time for responses differing from those opinons. If a televised editorial affects your company or your organization, ask for an opportunity to respond. As in radio, do not overlook the possibility of initiating positive editorials focusing on your company or organization.

Many local television stations will often provide free air

time to nonprofit organizations for timely, significant, and professionally produced public service announcements. Check with your local station manager for the specific requirements of each local entity.

NATIONAL RADIO OPPORTUNITIES

Most radio stations today have a clearly local orientation. Typically, they project themselves as independent media serving a specific local community. But there are very few that do not supplement programming by taking advantage of the vast array of news, information, and programming materials supplied by national radio networks, news services, and syndicates.

Here again, technologically advanced delivery systems such as satellites and microwave transmissions are encouraging the entry of new national news and programming services to feed the information-hungry radio audiences of America.

Again, as competition heats up and diversity rules, there are more and more opportunities for the message of your company or organization to get the ear of America through one or more of the following vehicles.

Commerical Radio Networks

Mention the word "network" and the images that most quickly come to mind are the familiar logos of the "Big Three" commercial networks: ABC, CBS and NBC. These three were the pioneers of broadcast; today they still are the giants of radio and television, providing thousands of broadcast stations with high quality news, information and programming geared to national interests.

But any survey of national network radio opportunities will identify more networks than the "Big Three." In fact, more than twenty commercial radio networks are thriving on the airwaves of America. Some are under the umbrellas of major communications giants. ABC, for example, has a half-dozen radio networks, each carefully targeted to a specific demographic audience. Some, like Mutual Broadcasting System, have been on the radio scene for decades. Others, like RKO Radio Networks, are relative newcomers.

Opportunities for news and feature stories about your company or organization on this diverse assortment of commercial radio networks are endless. But it takes concentrated effort and dedication to identify those opportunities and decide which of the many outlets are right for you.

It's an effort well worth making. If your story is aired on CBS Radio, for example, it will reach more than 500 local stations with a combined listening audience of millions. APR (Associated Press Radio) provides news and feature material to over 1,000 affiliates. UPI Audio feeds a network of over 1,400 radio stations. Audience figures for other networks are similarly impressive.

You can identify the many news and feature opportunities open to you on commercial networks through careful study of the resource materials described in Chapter Three, or by working with your local affiliated stations or regional bureaus (a technique also covered in Chapter Three).

National Public Radio

Unlike the commercial networks, which are profit-making corporations sustained by advertising revenues, National Public Radio (NPR) is a national programming service owned and governed by the nation's independent local radio stations. NPR is financed by the federal government and private grants and gifts. Its in-depth news reports and magazine-type shows have a serious public affairs orientation. Its audience is generally upscale, educated, and loyal.

Companies or organizations with credible, knowledgeable personnel who can speak authoritatively on topics of current interest or concern should become acquainted with the attractive opportunities presented by NPR.

Other Radio Networks

A vast array of regional networks should be included in any survey of the radio network opportunities available to your company or organization. These provide news and feature material to subscribing local radio stations in specific geographic areas (Midnight Sun Broadcasters), or within limited subject areas (Alamo Farm Network). *Broadcasting Yearbook* (see Chapter Three) has a complete listing of these highly specialized outlets.

If your company or organization is interested in getting its message to people in other nations, don't overlook Radio Free Europe, or the foreign radio networks, many of which have bureaus at the United Nations headquarters in New York City. The United Nations publishes a yearly guide listing every foreign news bureau and foreign correspondent in the country and how each may be contacted.

Radio News Services

Whether or not your local station is affiliated with a commercial network, it probably subscribes to at least one of the prolific news services that provide a steady stream of news, feature material, and special programming to the radio broadcast studios of America.

One of the biggest, with well over 3,000 radio stations subscribing, is the Associated Press Broadcasting News. Operating by wire, AP Broadcast transmits hourly national news reports, regional news, farm, business and stock market reports, news analyses and special feature material twenty-four hours a day from its national headquarters in Washington and dozens of regional bureaus across the country. United Press International Broadcast Newswire offers a similar service to thousands of local radio station subscribers here and abroad.

Both AP and UPI provide their reports in a script format, to be read by local broadcasters at each station. The scripts are termed "rip and read" because they are written in broadcast style—ready for the local announcer to "rip" off the wire transmitter, then "read" live on the air. In addition, both provide an audio service to subscribers.

You can work directly with the rip and read editors if you have a story of national news impact, and if you can write it in professional broadcast style (see Chapter Five). UPI's rip and read service is conducted out of Chicago, AP's out of Washington.

Reuters and Dow Jones are among other broadcast wire services widely used by local stations. Both emphasize stock market reports and analyses, business and financial reports, multipart series on taxes, investments and other personal finance topics.

Syndicated Programming

Other outlets for a story of national interest may be found in a variety of syndicated radio programs, produced privately and marketed to stations across the country. Many accept guests; some will do interviews by phone. Several have been popular supplements to local radio programming for many years and are subscribed to by hundreds of stations around the country. Subjects can vary from cooking and nutrition to home repairs, car maintenance, financial advice or beauty tips. Some syndicated programs are very brief, lasting thirty, sixty or ninety seconds; others may be fifteen or thirty minute segments or longer. Most are receptive to newsworthy ideas proposed by public relations professionals. Use your reference library to identify appropriate and meaningful syndicated opportunities for your company or organization.

NATIONAL TELEVISION OPPORTUNITIES

Time has always been a precious commodity on national television. To be considered for a nationally televised segment, your story must be especially significant, innovative, provocative, and timely. National television does not deal in trivia.

On the other hand, fine national television opportunities are more abundant than ever.

No longer are the half-hour network news program and a handful of morning and weekend talk shows the sole national television outlets for your story. Instead, twenty-four hour news programming offered via cable is winning the plaudits of television critics and audiences. Dozens of regional and national cable networks, many targeted to specific types of audiences, provide literally endless television opportunities for you on original news and feature programs. As in radio, ABC, CBS, and NBC are being challenged by a variety of independent networks that have assembled national news teams and are assertively competing for a share of time on the tube. The Big Three are responding by expanding their own news and feature coverage—earlier in the morning, later at night, during the day, on weekends.

This unprecedented explosion of national television outlets has some very practical consequences for the public relations professional. Audiences once glued to ABC, CBS and NBC are now more scattered and diffused. The mass television audience is being divided as more viewers abandon the networks to sample the variety of alternatives on the television screens today.

This "demassification" may make it more difficult than ever to find, reach, and measure a national television audience. Yet, because the number of television outlets has expanded so dramatically, there are many more opportunities for the adventurous, hard working public relations professional to pursue in order to communicate the story or message of his or her company or organization.

So whatever the difficulties or the challenges, don't discount the potential today for your story to achieve coverage on national television, and the prestige when it does. Following are some vehicles you might consider in identifying appropriate national outlets.

Commercial Television Networks

A variety of challengers are making inroads into what was once considered their exclusive turf—the mass television audience. Their shares of the total audience "glued to the tube" at any given moment continues a downward slide. But the three major networks, ABC, CBS, and NBC are still unsurpassed for their ability to reach, entertain, and inform television audiences numbering millions of Americans.

Partly in response to growing competition, the networks are producing more news and information programming than ever before. That means more opportunities than ever for your company or organization to communicate its message to a mass audience larger than can be reached by any other means.

Network headquarters are in New York, or you can work through the local network affiliates or regional bureaus in your area. (See Chapter Three.) Here are some national network formats to consider.

1. *Network News.* A national television news segment is still the crème de la crème of media opportunity for the message of your company or organization. Of all the myriad broadcast opportunities, a segment on network evening news, in prime time, presented by nationally known and respected broadcast journalists, still tops the list of prime targets for the most sophisticated public relations practitioner. Nothing else quite matches the prestige your story will attain if it is one of the handful chosen for coverage by one of these three selective, elusive outlets.

When you think network news however, don't just think of the prime time newscasts. Explore your resource books and your newspaper's television listings to get a fix on other national news opportunities. You will find news and information programming offered by networks periodically throughout the broadcast day and night. You will also find alternative news programming broadcast by independent ad hoc networks, formed by groups of independent local stations not affiliated with ABC, CBS or NBC.

When you have a story with national impact, or when that story has a very strong, very evident human interest angle, you may have an opportunity for that rare network news placement.

2. *News Documentaries.* The success and popularity of the CBS investigative news magazine "Sixty Minutes" has led to a

new emphasis on in-depth examination of current news and current issues by the networks. If your company or organization plays a key role in a program or a controversy of national importance, and if you can supply a knowledgeable, articulate authority, you may succeed in interesting the producers of a news magazine, a documentary, or an issue-oriented public affairs program in your topic. Before pursuing those opportunities, of course, be sure your company or organization is prepared to deal with tough, probing, aggressive broadcast journalists. (See Chapter Nine for interview guidelines.)

3. *Talk Shows.* For decades, the morning network talk show magazines, pioneered by NBC's "Today" in 1951, have set a standard for lively, provocative news/discussion/interview formats on national television. Still as lively and competitive today, the network morning programs provide outstanding opportunities for timely, innovative suggestions from your company or organization.

Other feature opportunities abound on network television for the imaginative and creative public relations professional who is alert for them. Magazine shows, early morning or late night talk programs, and even game shows can be suitable formats for an appearance by a spokesperson representing your company or organization. (See Chapter Six for formatting tips.)

Public Television

Headquartered in New York, the Educational Broadcasting Corporation is the major source of programming distributed nationally to some 250 educational television stations by the Public Broadcasting System (PBS). Like public radio, PBS is noncommercial, and financed by the government and by private and corporate grants. It offers in-depth news and information, as well as programming with an artistic and cultural orientation, to a well-educated, upscale, and faithful audience.

Public television stations across the country maintain strong, close ties. Major programs are taped in a variety of cities—San Francisco, Baltimore, Chicago, Boston—and supplied for airing on the national network. See your contact books (Chapter Three) to identify the sources of programs that interest you.

Cable Networks

Until recently, the commercial networks and public broadcasting were the "only game in town" for the public relations practitioner seeking a nationally televised format for the story or message of his or her company or organization. Now cable is revolutionizing national television, offering a burgeoning menu of news, talk, and information programming on a variety of ad sponsored and pay channels.

Some are calling cable the "magazine" of broadcasting because, like the proliferating print publications, many national cable networks and cable programmers are targeting very narrow, very specialized audiences—minorities, senior citizens, those interested in health and science, in medicine, even in weather reports. In some cases, cable programs are actual video versions of successful print publications like *Playboy*, *House and Garden*, and *Money*.

This new diversity of nationally televised cable networks presents its own set of challenges. To use these opportunities effectively, public relations professionals need to learn how to identify and segment their audiences, much as advertisers do. Consider who makes up your target audience (i.e., housewives between eighteen and thirty-five, teens, senior citizens, sports lovers), and then investigate which cable networks are targeted to that audience and what specific programs on those networks offer opportunities for your story idea.

Complicating this task is the very novelty and instability of the cable industry. New cable networks are proliferating, and new programming is introduced almost weekly. Some shows and some networks will thrive, and others will fail. It is still an entrepreneurial undertaking, with great risks for those who are getting in on the ground floor. There's still a shakedown process; the dust hasn't settled. But getting involved in the challenges and risks of this emerging industry is an exciting, absorbing, and rewarding aspect of broadcast public relations.

Syndicated Programming and Services

A growing number of independent production houses are making their presence felt in the expanded media marketplace of national television. Some produce widely viewed entertainment programs with talk show formats. Hosts and hostesses like Merv Griffin, David Susskind, Mike Douglas, and Phil Donahue have become household names. Although their formats are often geared toward light entertainment, a creatively presented idea proposed by your company or organization may find a warm reception.

Other syndicators are providing a variety of services designed to supplement the existing programming on the growing number of independent and cable stations. Some produce very short features, special reports, commentaries or interviews which are fed to purchasing stations by satellite on a daily or weekly basis.

Other are syndicated news services, providing supplementary news gathering capabilities to hard pressed local stations. These produce and offer multipart news series on subjects of national interest, or localized coverage of important events in cities distant from the broadcast studios of local stations.

The bottom line for public relations practitioners who are seeking broadcast opportunities is this: You have a tiger by the tail. There are more opportunities in radio and television than ever before, *but* you have to work harder to track them down, and you must work smarter to use them effectively.

part two

THE
HOW
FOR THE PUBLIC RELATIONS
PROFESSIONAL

chapter three

Contacting
the Decision Makers

Personal contact is the essence of good public relations. You cannot conduct a meaningful public relations program from behind your desk, or married to your telephone or your typewriter.

So, get out of your office. Meet and get to know your local broadcasters. Join the organizations they belong to, such as Sigma Delta Chi, Radio TV News Directors Association, the National Academy of Television Arts and Sciences, or Women in Communications. Go to the functions those groups and others sponsor. Take a tour of your local radio or television station. Invite a local anchorman or newscaster to tour your plant or visit a program your organization is proud of. Invite a local reporter for breakfast, lunch, or drinks. Invite him or her to speak at a function sponsored by your company or your organization. Get the dialogue going.

Learn the story needs and special requirements of the broadcast media, especially your local station's personnel. Know their "hot buttons"—the kind of stories that really get them excited. Know and understand their unique deadlines, and then respect those deadlines. Establish a reputation as a credible source of news and information, and your company or organization will find lots of good broadcast opportunities available to you.

TOOLS OF THE TRADE

Every company or organization with an interest in broadcast public relations should invest in a library of basic tools of the trade. There are many excellent publications available. Following are some of the best.

Annual Publications

BROADCASTING YEARBOOK   Some call it "the broadcaster's bible." It provides quantities of current information on the electronic media, listing every radio and television station in the country with such pertinent data as network affiliation, format (for radio stations), and the names of key personnel, from station manager to news director and program director. The *Broadcasting Yearbook* supplies names, addresses, and telephone numbers for those stations, as well as for regional networks, Radio Free Europe, television production houses, syndicates, and scores of other members of the broadcast community.

NATIONAL RADIO PUBLICITY DIRECTORY   This lists some 1,800 talk shows on radio stations across the country, with such data as format, air time, tape time, target audiences and names of persons to contact who work directly with each show. It is a very helpful supplement to the radio section of *Broadcasting Yearbook*, especially when you want to contact radio programs outside your local area.

TV PUBLICITY OUTLETS NATIONWIDE   Some 1,300 television programs across the country, including local, network and nationally syndicated programs are listed, providing names of contact personnel at each.

If you're interested in cable (and you should be), a number of directories for the cable industry are being or will soon be introduced into the marketplace. These can be expected to multiply in the coming years and should surely have a place as invaluable resources in your public relations library.

Although these resources and directories are revamped once a year, do not assume every contact name at every station or program is the correct, current contact. Broadcast is a mobile business, people move rapidly from job to job, station to station, city to city. If you're working in unfamiliar turf, it always pays to pick up the phone and make sure you have the right name before you make a key contact.

Periodicals for Current Information

BROADCASTING MAGAZINE A weekly publication, this keeps the industry updated on technological developments, current issues, controversies, industry meetings, special events, and format and programming innovations and changes. In its "Fates and Fortunes" section, it offers timely information about people to contact in the industry, and announces appointments, promotions, and changes.

VARIETY Another industry staple, in both daily and weekly form, this has a radio and television section that many public relations professionals consider "must reading" due to its complete coverage of broadcast news and its upbeat writing.

TV GUIDE This weekly publication offers much more than your local television listings. It is also the source of some of the most insightful and knowledgeable commentary on the television industry available today.

MEDIA NEWS KEYS, PR AIDS PARTY LINE, LARIMI CONTACTS These are weekly newsletters with nationwide updates on programs, formats, and personnel. They will often provide you with inside information on current programming plans at broadcast networks and stations across the country. If your company has affiliations in a distant city, a local talk show in that area may be planning a special series that would be just the right setting for the story you want to tell.

A well-planned reference library, kept updated, will prove invaluable to you in building contacts with the broadcast media.

ASSEMBLING A MEDIA TARGET LIST

Buying books and subscribing to periodicals is just the beginning. Public relations, as we'll say again and again, is a personal contact business. Your reference library will not be complete until you personalize those reference books by making contact with the decision makers at the stations and the programs where you hope to arrange some air time for your company or your organization.

Use your reference library as a starting point and go on from there. Start your own file on three by five cards or on a rolodex. Choose any method that's comfortable for you. Don't just copy names out of a book or a newsletter. Make personal or telephone contact with those names. And gradually, slowly, sometimes painfully, you will assemble a meaningful media target list for your company or organization.

Local Contacts

Day in and day out, your local broadcast stations are the most fertile and most essential outlets for the news and features generated by your company or organization. That's good. Because usually they are also the most accessible.

Your local broadcasters want to know you—and want to know about your company or organization—because they are in the business of reporting local news and information. You represent an organization that is most probably a vital economic and/or social force in your town or city. Broadcasters want and need to know about everything that affects the lives and fortunes of the people in the community. You need them to tell your story effectively; they need you in order to do their jobs well.

As one broadcaster put it, "Public relations people are the extension of our ears and eyes." Get to know the local broadcast scene and the people who make it work, and you will soon develop pipelines in the newsrooms and broadcast studios of your own community. Eventually, you'll be commanding some very meaningful air time for your company or organization.

Those are generalities. Following are some specifics.

TARGET STATION-BY-STATION   You're new in town. Or you're new on the job. Or your company has looked askance at radio or television interview requests in the past; now someone in the executive suite has decided that was a mistake. Now the company wants air time. And you've been put in charge.

One approach is to build your local media target list station-by-station. Consult your reference books and your local telephone directory to compile a list of every radio and television station located in or broadcast in your community. Do not overlook the cable outlets—they are valuable contacts offering multiple broadcast opportunities—and most likely their personnel will be eager to know you and work with you.

Make a complete list. Then, get on the phone. Contact someone at each and every station on your list—the station manager, the news or program director, or the reporter who specializes in your area, whether it be business, education, health, science, sports, or consumer information. Introduce yourself. Tell him or her something about your company or organization. Explain that you are interested in providing news and information on a regular basis. If you can, make an appointment to visit the station in person or for an introductory breakfast or lunch.

Your initial call or visit is really a fact finding mission. You want to learn as much as you can about that station, the programming it is most proud of, and the people who work there. Without playing "Twenty Questions" (broadcasters, like you, are busy people), you will be looking for such information as:

- Who are the key decision makers at the station?
- How much do they know about your company or organization, your field or industry?
- What are the deadlines for news? For feature ideas?
- When is the best time to contact the assignment editor? The beat reporter? The talent on the station's talk shows?
- When should you call? When should you send a letter?
- Will the (radio) station use an audio feed if you provide a newsworthy one? Is the (television) station interested in getting file footage you have shot at your plant or facility?
- What special programming plans (documentaries, news feature series, talk show themes) are in the works?
- Does the station have personnel available for on-location interviews? (Many smaller stations rarely do.)

Be interested and observant. Keep careful, complete notes. Write down the correctly spelled name of every person you meet or speak to. Be aware of the way each broadcaster seems to approach the job, and his or her special interests or expertise. If someone has been especially helpful or informative, follow-up with a short note expressing your appreciation.

Start a dialogue with someone at each local broadcast station, and you will soon begin to recognize the many opportunities each outlet offers you and your company or organization.

TARGET PROGRAM-BY-PROGRAM   Another effective approach to getting to know your local broadcast media is to make your own personal survey of the radio and television programs that air in your community. Study those local newspaper listings. Watch and listen to as many broadcast programs as you can throughout the day. When you go home at night or as you drive across town, don't fall into the rut of turning to the same old station. Try something new. Flip that dial. Be alert for programs—a morning drive time broadcast, a noon public affairs show, a call-in program, a Sunday evening news wrap—that might be potential outlets for your own company or organization. Listen with an ear and view with an eye toward where and how your material might fit in.

Become a careful, alert listener or viewer. Every station,

every program—even time slots within the same program—
have subtleties, nuances, and special areas of emphasis that will
offer some clues to the kinds of broadcast opportunities they
might provide for your story or interview idea. The disk
jockey who hosts your town's most popular radio station during
morning drive time may schedule an interview with a prominent local businessman or woman twice every week, while the
afternoon drive time broadcaster on the very same station seems
to plan programming around local sports personalities. A popular morning talk show that is broadcast in your town may have
a regular pattern of topics for its viewers. For instance, ten
minutes for local news, ten minutes for education, religion,
or charitable segments, five for sports, and five for a visiting
celebrity or a consumer how-to piece.

Local news coverage is not all the same. Each radio station
has a different emphasis; some rely heavily on their network
affiliates for news, some have aggressive reporters beating the
bushes for local stories, some have twenty-four hour news and
talk formats that offer plentiful forums for your company or
organization. Know the personality and the emphasis of each
radio news team in your community.

Local television news presents similar contrasts. Many
broadcasters see local news as the primary identity of the station
and its local news coverage sets the tone for how each station is
perceived in the community and the region. Thus, television
news broadcasts are highly competitive, yet each deliberately
aims to develop and portray a distinct personality, a unique
identity. If you are observant and perceptive, you will know
which news team is most likely to be there if you schedule a
morning news conference, who will be most interested in the
day care center you've opened for employees, and who will be
most skeptical, or aggressive, or open-minded when your company or organization gets involved in a controversial situation.

It is not enough, though, to merely hear and see what
everyone is doing. You also have to act. Contact those programs
that appear to offer some immediate opportunity to your company or spokesperson. If you hear a radio commentator who
loves to tell human interest stories, and your organization has
a "people story" to tell, call that broadcaster and introduce

yourself. Describe your idea. Tell him or her about the volunteer who's given up her Sunday nights every week for thirty years to work with youngsters in your community. Suggest an interview. You'll make a contact, and perhaps develop a mutually meaningful segment.

TARGET PERSON-BY-PERSON   Whether you began assembling your local media target list station-by-station, or program-by-program, the end result will be the same. It will all come down to people; meeting people face-to-face, getting to know them, and working with them. It cannot be said too often. Personal contact is the essence of good public relations. No matter what your message, or which company or organization you represent, there is no one right person to call when you have a story to tell. The best person to contact is the person you know.

As you meet and work with more and more of your local broadcasters, your network of contacts will widen faster than you could ever imagine. The anchorman you met at one station moves to another. The researcher for the morning talk show is promoted to assistant producer. The disk jockey who interviewed your CEO after the opening of your new plant becomes host of a syndicated public affairs talk show. All the while, you are part of the action, and you are in the mix. The time and energy you devoted to building those personal local contacts will all be evident in the priceless personal contact file that's bulging with names and notations on your desk, leading to valuable air time for you.

National Contacts

Not every story idea you generate or every news release you write will be of enough general interest to merit national coverage. But don't discount your potential for landing air time on national radio or television.

An all too common attitude among companies and organizations located at points distant from the Eastern Seaboard is that national broadcasters aren't interested in them because they

are so far away from the "communications capital," of New York. It's not true. Your location in the Midwest, South or Northern Pacific states can actually be an advantage. Most national broadcast journalists are anxious to avoid the reputation or even the appearance of being too tied to New York and Washington for their news and views. They want to know, and show they know, what's going on in other parts of the nation—how people west of the Hudson and Potomac Rivers are dealing with the issues and concerns of the day.

The desire for broad and balanced coverage is one reason you may well find national newsmakers unexpectedly receptive to a good broadcast idea, especially if it's proposed in a professional and helpful manner. As one talent coordinator for a network morning program told a gathering of public relations people at an industry seminar: "We are crying for help and we just don't get enough of it. We need contacts throughout the country; we need good stories from middle America. So help us, flood us, and don't give up if your first idea doesn't fly. We really do need you."

There is another reason why national broadcasters are more willing than ever to consider an idea that's generated at points distant from their broadcast studios. Advances in technology like satellite transmission and portable mini-cams have made it more feasible and less costly to go where the action is and to cover good stories wherever they occur.

There are a variety of approaches to making contact with the national broadcast media. Following are some you might consider.

LOCAL AFFILIATES   It is not always necessary to work long distance, with unfamiliar names and faces, in order to obtain national coverage of your story. Instead work with someone you already know: the local broadcast journalist at a network affiliated station in your own community.

A manufacturer successfully completed experiments with a new wastewater treatment process in a mid-sized Michigan city. The environmental editor at a network affiliate in town got interested in the story and saw its national implications. Rather than just shooting one version of the story, he edited a second version for the network's nightly news feed. That night, a segment on the new wastewater treatment process was made available to all the network affiliates, via the nightly news feed. A local story was edited and got national play.

The secondary feed is the network news show you and I never see. All three television (and radio) networks run a secondary feed every night—a selection of 10 or 12 stories, often supplied by local affiliates, that didn't make it on the network news program, but are still considered to have national impact. Every local affiliate can receive the feed and has the option of incorporating part or all of it into its local programming.

Not every station will air every segment that's supplied via the secondary feed. Each subscribing station picks up the items that appear to have some local interest. But if just one third of the network affiliates had aired the wastewater treatment segment, viewers of forty or fifty stations would have seen the piece. And that's national coverage.

REGIONAL BUREAUS Every radio and television network maintains several strategically placed regional bureaus, serving every geographic area within the nation. The job of the bureau personnel is to "enterprise" stories—to find out and report what's happening in Maine and Georgia, in Kansas and New Mexico. If your company or organization has an interesting story to tell, the regional bureau reporters want to know you. In most cases, they will become your most steady national contacts.

"Boredom on the job" was a national concern. Nearly every magazine and newscast had its story about how workers were getting tired of just turning the same widget eight hours a day. An office machine company with a plant in a small southern town was conducting an experiment to combat the problem. Instead of the typical assembly line operation, workers were turning out complete office machines from the first turn of the screw to the last. The project was described to a reporter at a network bureau in Atlanta. Within the week, a camera crew filmed the story and it aired on the nightly network news. Not only was it a piece of favorable corporate news, but it turned out to be a terrific piece of product publicity.

You can find out where your nearest regional bureaus are located by calling the local network affiliates in your own home town, or by consulting your reference library. Then make some calls, just as you did when you began the task of building your local contacts. Introduce yourself. Find out if there's a reporter or correspondent who specializes in your field or industry. If the nearest bureau is 100 miles from your office, but you're planning a business trip in that direction, try to arrange an appointment to visit with that reporter in person.

Of course, your contact will always be most effective when it's backed up by a timely, newsworthy story idea. If your plant is located in Charleston and your engineers have developed a new method for low cost solar air conditioning, that's a fine time to get in touch with the network bureaus in the southeast. Let them know something exciting is happening on their beat. They'll welcome your call. You are helping them do their job. Once you have established bureau contacts, you will have created another fruitful avenue for meaningful air time for your company or your organization.

MAKING CONTACT DIRECTLY   Local affiliates and regional bureaus can be excellent and effective pipelines into the national broadcast studios of America. On the other hand, those same national studios are as near as the telephone on your desk, or the stationery in your typewriter.

If you are convinced you have a story that's just right for "Good Morning America" or an interview that can only be done, in your view, by Jane Pauley or Diane Sawyer, there is no reason why you can't reach for your typewriter or pick up your phone and make those contacts directly. Adopt the same techniques you are already using so effectively with your own local broadcasters. It's probably safe to say that just about every broadcast journalist who has made it to the top at the networks got his or her start at a small station, perhaps in a town somewhat like yours. They may have more material to choose from now, and therefore be more selective, but they still know a good idea when they hear one. And if you are the one to offer that "just right" idea, they'll be happy to hear from you and will work with you to get that story on air.

You can use your reference library to zero in on the right national show and the right person to contact at that show. In some cases, you can watch the credits at the end of the show, and choose a name from those. It may take some patience and effort before you find the right person, but if you believe in your story, stick with it. There are few accomplishments in broadcast public relations more satisfying than arranging an effective broadcast segment for your company or organization on a major network program.

PUTTING YOUR MEDIA
TARGET LIST TO WORK

There are some public relations people who have compiled the most extensive, up-to-date, personalized media lists one could ever hope for. They have lunch twice a week with someone from the broadcast media. They know all about George's "hot buttons"; they belong to all the right organizations and even work on committees and go to meetings. But nothing much happens. Their company or organization never seems to get the air time that ought to result from all that activity.

To accomplish your goal of meaningful air time, you have to put that media target list to work for you. You have to know your company or organization inside out. You have to be alert for the broadcast potential in every activity that takes place in your plant, every new program, anniversary, special event, contest or new product. Then you have to shape those rough ideas into meaningful proposals (see Chapter Six), and get those proposals out, at the right time, to the right people, in the right form.

If you have a good story idea, don't just send a letter to one person and sit back and wait for something to happen. At any one time, you should have five or six or more different ideas out on the street to all the broadcasters you think will be interested.

There are lots of valid reasons why a perfectly good story idea doesn't fly. Perhaps a similar story is already "in the can," or the show you're aiming for is devoting the month to a special theme, or the station can't spare a crew to visit your site at the time you've planned your special event.

But one rejection is not a reason to give up or sit back. It's the reason why you have to work harder. If you keep trying, you *will* connect, not just once, but again and again.

chapter four

Working with Broadcasters

Why does the evening news reporter need my home phone number? Why did the crew shoot at our plant for half a day and only thirty seconds made it to air? Why are those assignment editors so abrupt on the phone? Why doesn't the producer return my phone call? Why did they cancel my interview at the last minute? Why do they insist I answer their questions now when the news isn't on for four more hours? Why did they promise to come to our news conference and never show up? Why are their reports so shallow? Why are they more interested in drama, controversy and entertainment than in careful news analysis? Don't they care about telling the whole story?

The broadcast journalist! He or she doesn't operate in the familiar pattern of your local newspaper reporter or the editor of the trade publications in your field.

The journalist and the public relations professional often approach a story or event from differing points of view. Sometimes, their viewpoints can be adversarial. The journalist is primarily concerned with getting the story. The executive and public relations professional have two concerns: telling the story *and* positioning it to reflect equitably on the company or organization.

Most people in business and nonprofit organizations who care about good public relations have come across this potentially adversarial relationship with *print* journalists, and have come to terms with it. They have developed a rapport, or at least an uneasy truce with the print reporters with whom they deal regularly. When a newspaper reporter calls or a magazine writer requests an interview, the organization responds factually and accurately. Public relations professionals respect deadlines, try to provide information when it's needed, and work hard to keep the lines of communication open.

It is just as important, and perhaps more so in this electronic age, to keep open and build those lines of communication between your company or organization and the broadcasters of your community. But it may require more effort and more initiative on your part. Don't wait passively for broadcasters to begin acting more like the print journalists you're accustomed to, because they won't.

Instead, make an effort to understand the special demands on, and the professional needs of, broadcast journalists. Try to "get inside their heads" to see why they work the way they do. Your initiative will make it far easier to develop productive, mutually beneficial channels of communication between your office and the radio and television studios or newsrooms of your community.

Here are some guidelines to help you work more cordially and effectively with broadcast decision makers.

RESEARCH IN ADVANCE

The economics of sending a correspondent and camera crew to cover a story or event are quite different from the cost of sending a reporter with a pencil. A recent estimate: it costs between $1000 and $1500 to put a news crew (one sound and one camera crew member) on the street each day.

Further, the logistics of taping a television story, even with advanced equipment like portable mini-cameras, impose further restrictions on broadcasters. It simply takes longer to move, set up, and take down those television cameras and lights. The average news crew, therefore, can cover just two or

Even more important, develop a real feel for the story, be able to envision how it will play on radio or television.

Whenever possible, it is best to get your information first-hand. If the story you are proposing is happening in Little Rock, then go to Little Rock. Research it for yourself; do some homework. Get your facts directly from the source. Take a cassette recorder with you or take careful notes. Be skeptical. Ask questions.

> A building supplies manufacturer and a utility joined to create experimental "super thermal homes" with insulation double the usual thickness. Studies of the experimental homes showed the insulation substantially reduced heating and cooling costs. But rather than proposing a story based on statistics, the public relations professional took time to visit the site and conduct dozens of interviews with those who had developed and studied the project, and those who bought and lived in the homes.
>
> This thorough preparation paid off. The first-hand information and the enthusiasm it generated brought two network television news teams to the site to film the experimental dwellings. These two high visibility segments helped encourage consumers to understand the value of the company's product and were effective image enhancers for the utility company.

Careful research can improve your credibility as a resource *and* increase your own enthusiasm about your story. Conversely, it will prevent you from wasting broadcasters' time and money with trivia or misleading them with inaccurate information. We have an obligation to make sure we are supplying our media contacts with truthful, accurate, and complete information. Be sure your story is legitimate and is suitable for broadcast before you suggest it.

Know Your Spokesperson

You may succeed once—on the basis of a friendship with a broadcast decision maker or by virtue of your own sales ability or enthusiasm—in arranging a radio or television interview with a dull, evasive, or inarticulate spokesperson for your company or organization.

Enjoy watching that interview! It is probably the last time you'll ever succeed in interesting that broadcaster in your ideas.

Radio and television rely on drama and energy to attract and hold the attention of their audiences. Producers can't afford tedium and can't let the pace drag. When you suggest a broadcast interview, implicitly you're assuming responsibility for providing a spokesperson who can speak for your company or organization forthrightly, clearly, and with enthusiasm.

This doesn't mean you must limit your spokespersons to performers, extroverts, or trained public speakers. To the contrary. The most effective interview is often with the individual who is most closely connected to the story or message being conveyed, the one who can bring real authenticity, insight and authority to the interview.

It does mean you are obligated to make sure your spokesperson is well-prepared for the broadcast interview and that he or she has the ability to handle the responsibility comfortably. Guidelines for choosing and preparing a spokesperson are the topic of Chapter Nine.

Suggest an Approach

The right show, a well-prepared, articulate spokesperson and a solid story idea are all essential ingredients in a successful broadcast public relations project. In some cases, they may be enough to get that story on air.

But your success ratio will increase dramatically if you take the time to walk the extra mile—if you can suggest not only a story, but an angle, and approach to the story. A broadcast segment, even a ninety-second interview, is a carefully constructed package. It must appeal to eyes and ears as well as intellect. For television, think about visuals you can build on to convey and enhance your message. For radio, an audio tape may offer that special attention grabber that will give your story idea its added interest for the broadcast audience.

A spokesperson for a nonprofit organization was suggested for an interview on a major market radio talk show. The organ ization had been the subject of a popular feature film several years earlier. An audio tape of a famous line from the film was offered to the station, and that line provided the takeoff point for a lively and heartwarming radio interview heard by thousands of listeners.

When you take the trouble to identify and research a suitable format for your idea, you'll win extra points with harried broadcasters. Some professionals go so far as to recommend a spokesperson with an opposing viewpoint to help balance the segment they are suggesting. That's impressive, and effective, public relations.

Sometimes, people think they must have professional broadcast experience in order to develop or "format" a successful radio or television segment. That's not necessary. We are all amateur producers. If you watch and listen to television and radio with a critical ear and eye, you will soon develop your own sensitivities to the angles and approaches to shape your story ideas into effective broadcast segments. Chapter Six suggests many do-able ideas to harness your creativity and point you in the right direction.

PERSONALIZE EVERY CONTACT

The days of mass distribution of a broadcast story idea are over. Probably, they ended years ago. But too many public relations people, in agencies, corporations and nonprofit organizations, continue to send those mass produced, depersonalized, general letters and "press kits" with the idea that quantity may substitute for quality.

Resist that impulse. Don't take the easy way out. Public relations is a personal contact business. Broadcasters, like anyone, want to be treated as individuals, not as a member of a large, anonymous mass. Some editors automatically throw away word-processed letters or addressographed envelopes. They know when they are getting one piece of a mass mailing.

Make every letter a personal letter. Don't send it to a

station or a program. Send it to a person, and make sure it's the right person. If you are not sure, take the time to call in advance. Is John Brown still producing "Local News Tonight"? Is "Women in Action" still broadcast every Sunday night?

Radio and television are mobile career fields. Some public relations people fail to keep abreast of frequent changes in stations' broadcasting personnel. "I still get letters addressed to the woman who had my job two years ago," is a frequent lament among radio and television decision makers.

Once you are sure you have the right name, be sure you spell it correctly (a common courtesy all too often overlooked). Don't give your office the reputation of a mass mailout house. Don't play the numbers game. Write personalized, customized, individualized letters and story proposals. Be careful and courteous enough to address them properly. Come up with different, carefully targeted angles. Show in your letter that you're aware of what the broadcaster is doing and what he or she needs. Show the person receiving it that you intended it just for him or her.

RECOGNIZE THE IMPORTANCE OF TIME

In radio and television, time is all-important. It's not that broadcasters are busier, more harried or pressured than other people. We can all legitimately say we are victims of those conditions. But in broadcast, everything is measured in minutes and seconds. The radio news broadcast must last the prescribed five minutes, or seven, or ten—not a second more or a second less. The television interview must be timed exactly according to predetermined limits, so the program can begin and end exactly on schedule.

As we have already seen, the distilled, abbreviated, condensed format of broadcast news and information presentation is a direct result of constraints imposed by time. There are only sixty minutes to an hour, twenty-four hours to a day. Fast paced programming of short, varied segments to entertain and hold the attention of listener and viewer is the mainstay of radio and television formats.

"We're not educators. We don't have time to teach," says a radio news producer from a major market station. "We can only go to the obvious—then create a climate that will spark people's interest in a subject."

Developing a true understanding of the absolute limits time imposes on your associates in broadcasting is an important prerequisite to working with them effectively. Following are some specific things to do.

Plan Enough Lead Time

If you have an important, urgent, "breaking" news story to tell, forget about lead time. Pick up the phone and call. Radio and television are instant media. Broadcasters cherish their reputation of being first on the scene and work hard to be available for quick response when it is required. They will appreciate your help.

In public relations, though, most story ideas are not of the urgent "hard news" variety. They are feature ideas, "soft" stories, back of the book suggestions. When you are suggesting a feature idea—an interview with your Chief Executive Officer, a segment on your new volunteer program—allow plenty of lead time.

Make your initial contact at least two or three weeks in advance. That allows the broadcaster time to consider your idea, research it, construct an appealing format, integrate it with other pending segments, schedule studio time or arrange for a reporter and a crew to shoot on location, prepare a working script and attend to the dozens of myriad details that are required before your story hits air.

In larger markets and/or for very popular shows, you may find the necessary lead time is even longer than two or three weeks. That's one question you should ask when you begin making those all-important personal contacts at your local broadcast stations (See Chapter Three). Conversely, your idea may be so timely or may be so well suited to a program theme currently under development that you'll find the cameras at your door the day your letter arrives.

Watch Your Scheduling

The timing of your story can be a significant factor in how much air time it gets. This is especially true when you're targeting those highly visible television nightly news programs in your community (or on the networks).

Be aware, first of all, of the three to four hours of back-time required to get a story ready for air, and to script and edit it into its final form. "Every news segment is like a mini-novel," according to a veteran television news producer. "You have to build the story carefully. That takes time and effort by lots of people." Back-time means if you want television news cameras at your news conference, you'd better not schedule it late in the day. Because of back-time, if you're asked to respond to a breaking story about a crisis in your organization and you haven't done so by midafternoon, the "Six O'Clock News" may legitimately report that you had "no comment."

On the other hand, a newsworthy story proposal made on a "light" news day may merit more than the usual air time. Consider planning your special event on a weekend or a Monday morning, when the news flow tends to be slower, for maximum broadcast results. Contact business correspondents on days when the stock market is closed and there may be less competition from other financial news sources. Call the night editor at your local radio station late in the evening and offer a taped actuality about a current issue for airing on drive time the following morning. (See Chapter Eight for how-to.) He or she may find your story a welcome change from the endless stream of crime and tragedy news items that are so often the steady fare of the overnight news crew.

It's just as important, for your own efficiency and effectiveness, to be aware of the individual schedules and availability of the broadcasters at your local stations. This is mostly a matter of getting to know them personally and finding out how they work. But there are a few generalizations that apply quite universally. Usually, you shouldn't count on making contact with a television news reporter if you have a hot story requiring an instant response. Generally, news correspondents are not sitting at their desks in the news room all day. They are out on location, then locked into the editing room with a tape editor and a producer to format their stories right up until air time. They may not even get your message until the next morning. "Don't ever call me for lunch; I haven't eaten lunch in years," says one active consumer correspondent. "I do have breakfast, sometimes, but once I get to the studio, my life isn't my own."

Most news stories originate with an assignment editor. That individual is on the desk all day. Call early in the morning to propose a story for that day; if you want to discuss future news coverage, late afternoon is probably the best time. Don't overlook other broadcast decision makers either. You should get to know the schedules and availability of producers, news directors, and researchers at your local stations. Remember the on-air talent. Even though they are on the go, sometimes they are accessible and frequently wield real decision making power. If they like your story, they will find a way to do it.

Prepare Your People

It's not enough that *you* recognize the overwhelming impact of time pressures and deadlines on the broadcaster. Every person in your organization who will have any dealings with the radio and television decision makers of your community should be thoroughly briefed so they, too, understand how time limitations may affect the way broadcasters deal with your story.

If your vice president of finance is being interviewed on tape as part of a local documentary, he or she should be prepared to make brief, distilled responses that can be edited into twenty- or thirty-second "sound bites" without sacrificing accuracy or clarity (see Chapter Nine). He or she should not expect solicitous attention by the camera crew or interviewer. "In the early days, we used to take the time to warm the person up, and let him get used to the cameras and lights," says a network television newswoman. "Today, unless we're working with a small child, we just don't have the time. It's just point and shoot." Your vice president, therefore, must be prepared for cursory treatment, and be ready to respond instantly.

Conversely, your colleagues should know, in advance, that although the camera may roll for a half hour during your morning news conference, or a crew with an investigative reporter may spend a half day at your plant, only a small portion of that footage can be expected to air. It's your job to convey, not only the fact that the material will probably be distilled and edited, but *why* that will happen and *how* they can deal with that reality. Give your colleagues the information and insight they need to be effective in every broadcast situation.

BE FLEXIBLE

Whether you're in a small city or a major market, your story is always vulnerable to the erratic and ever-changing flow of the news. If your local assignment editor agrees to send a crew to your press conference, and a truck full of toxic chemicals overturns on the highway just outside of town, you may not ever see the cameras that day. If a feature about your new day care program is scheduled to air on the local news tonight and a four-alarm fire breaks out in your city's largest department store, that feature may be delayed, or may never be used at all.

You can't prevent those discouraging postponements and cancellations from happening. But you can be aware of the possibility, and be flexible enough to have an alternate plan. What will you do if the cameras don't show up at your morning news conference? Perhaps you can arrange to bring your top executive into the studio for an interview, or provide some broadcast-quality animation footage of the event along with a thirty-second piece of copy written especially for the broadcast medium (see Chapter Eight). Have a back-up plan. You will sometimes need it.

BE POLITELY PERSISTENT

If you have a story you believe in, stick with it until you find a receptive broadcast outlet for it. When you've done your homework, researched your story and the market and are convinced you have an airworthy idea, don't be discouraged by a rejection or two. Don't give up until you're sure you've exhausted all the possibilities.

> Under pressure to get national television exposure, a corporate public relations officer convinced producers of a network morning magazine show to send a film crew to a midwest location to film the opening of a new gallery that would house some of the world's great works of glass art. The sponsoring firm was elated. But at the eleventh hour, the filming was cancelled. The network decision makers had decided the costs of sending people and equipment to that out of the way location were just too high. Rather than just accepting that decision, this enterprising public relations person proposed an alternate plan which was accepted. A few choice pieces of art and the museum curator were flown to the New York network studios. The result was a successful live in-studio segment on a choice national television program.

Stick with your story, but don't be overly insistent. Perseverance and persistence pay, but being pushy does not. Think of long-term relationships and commitments when you propose your ideas. No story is worth risking future opportunities. Strive to maintain friendly and professional relationships with every broadcast decision maker you contact.

Remember, radio and television are increasingly competitive markets. When your story is good, there will be broadcast decision makers who will see its potential. If the first person or the first station you contact isn't receptive, try another. Then, later on, you can come back to the first contact with another idea.

That next time, if your original concept didn't sell, try a slightly different angle, a new peg. You'll be surprised how often just the smallest new twist in a story proposal will arouse the interest of an initially unreceptive broadcaster.

THINK NEWS

Today there are more broadcast outlets for news and information programming than ever before. The quantity and quality of those opportunities is growing faster every week, month, and year.

There's no single, universally accepted definition of "news" today. In fact, if you were to ask ten broadcasters what "news" is you'd probably get ten different definitions. Some say the only true news stories are those dealing with matters of national and international consequence. Some find little difference between news and entertainment, contending that news is "anything that interests people."

Rather than dwelling on finding a valid definition, it's probably best to accept the face that "news" is a broad category today. Just as your daily newspaper contains many items that are not late-breaking items of national and international consequence, so radio and television stations are expanding their definitions of news to include more feature material, more "back of the book" human interest segments.

That's good for you. Your company or organization is making news every day. Occasionally, your news may be of real interest and consequence to large numbers of people. More often, you'll have to make the extra effort needed to format and position your story to make it "airworthy."

That is the challenge, and the satisfaction, of effective broadcast public relations.

chapter five

Writing Broadcast Style

Writing for broadcast is different from writing for newspapers or magazines. Sentences are short. Words are simple.

Broadcast style is informal. It's conversational. Its meaning reaches the audience through the ear as well as the eye. As one prominent television newscaster described it, "It's one neighbor chatting to another over the backyard fence."

But writing for broadcast is far from a casual undertaking. It's a fine art, requiring precision, discipline, and practice. Each word is chosen carefully to catch and hold the listener's or viewer's attention while simultaneously communicating the essence of the story.

To get the feel of broadcast style, listen to an evening newscast on your favorite television network. Don't watch it; turn away and *listen*. You will hear short words, simple sentences and clear, direct communication.

The words spoken by Dan Rather, Tom Brokaw, or Peter Jennings might seem terse or jumpy if they appeared in your morning newspaper. On television or radio they sound easy, casual, and natural, and they tell the story.

TECHNIQUES OF BROADCAST STYLE

The techniques of writing for broadcast are specialized, and require years of practice to perfect. Radio and television stations employ trained personnel who make a career of writing for those media.

You need not develop the expertise of the head writers at ABC, CBS, NBC or CNN. But if you're aware of the elements of broadcast style, and incorporate them into your written communications with broadcasters, your message will have that important competitive edge in the media marketplace.

> A company hired a freelance magazine writer to prepare publicity material about a new educational program it had developed. The writer labored over a detailed five-page release for local newspapers and radio stations.
>
> Fortunately, the wordy document was intercepted by a co-worker who knew something about broadcast. He found a "lead" at the bottom of the third page, distilled the story to three paragraphs and sent it to several radio outlets, including a national broadcast wire service. Just two days later, that story was heard, word for word, in rip and read newscasts from coast to coast.

You can send the business editor of your local newspaper a copy of the newsmaking twenty-five page speech your board chairman will be making Thursday night. That editor might extract some quotes from it or use it as the basis of an interview. But if you send that same speech to a broadcast journalist, the envelope will probably never even be opened. Instead, send a short news release to your local radio newscaster, written broadcast style. Focus on the highlights of that speech, and the results will be worth the effort. You'll more than likely get that broadcaster's attention and perhaps an airing on morning drive time or the noon-day news report.

How do you translate a wordy or complicated story into broadcast style? Here are some basic guidelines.

Keep It Short

Distill! Abbreviate! Capsulize! Radio and television are condensed media. They're often called "headline services," or, as one newscaster quipped, "Cartoons with captions."

Broadcast newscasts are brief because they're restricted by time. A five-minute radio newscast may have as little as three and a half minutes of news. If eight stories are told, each must be communicated in less than thirty seconds. Most radio news directors try to include between eight and ten stories in each five-minute broadcast.

Similarly, a half-hour television news program has only about twenty-two minutes of news after you subtract time for the obligatory station break, for commercials and for transitions from news to commercial and back again.

In those twenty-two minutes, rating-conscious broadcasters must pick up the pace by airing ever shorter and shorter stories. As we've seen, the theory is that short pieces allow more stories, more variety and a quickened pace. Faster paced newscasts hold the viewers' attention, and will attract more viewers. In broadcasting, that's the name of the game.

The bottom line: Television news directors want most stories to average between seventy-five and ninety seconds. Radio stories, as we've seen, are even shorter. The average newscaster reads about 150 words of copy per minute. Figure it out for yourself. Then, *keep it short.*

Perhaps you're already starting to protest here. Your story is too complicated, or too important, or too technical to tell in 150 words. Not so! It can be done, effectively and accurately, with determination and practice.

Industries that rely on television advertising to keep sales booming manage to tell their stories in thirty seconds, and happily pay hundreds of thousands of dollars for the privilege. Similarly, the United Way and the Muscular Dystrophy Association, along with hundreds of other nonprofit organizations, have perfected the art of conveying messages effectively via thirty second public service announcements. You can meet that same challenge.

How do you start? Following are some hints.

ZERO IN ON THE ESSENCE OF YOUR STORY   The essence is the one word or phrase that best summarizes your message or the story you want to tell. Perhaps you'll find that key word or phrase in the lead of the news release you wrote for the local newspaper. You may find it "buried" halfway through the story. Perhaps it will only be implied. But wherever it is, find it, and start there.

NO: Members of all five churches in Highland Hills will gather Sunday for an evening of song, dance, good food and fellowship . . .

YES: Old time religion! It returns Sunday to Highland Hills when . . .

The short, abbreviated, vivid opening grabs the attention of the listener or viewer. And getting attention is the basic essential of broadcasting writing. Here's another example:

NO: George Ellis, chairman of the XYZ Plastics Corporation, has just returned from Europe where, he says, plastics are easily burned in clean, modern incinerators.

YES: Plastics! How can we dispose of them? Some say we can't. George Ellis says we can.

If you can't think of a single word or brief phrase that summarizes your story, maybe you just haven't thought hard enough. Read it again, and keep trying.

USE THE "SOFT" LEAD   Journalistic tradition tells us to include all the basic facts in the first paragraph of the story—those traditional "five W's"—who, what, when, where and why. In broadcast, that's almost always poor advice. Don't try to get too much information into one sentence. Instead, try the "soft lead":

NO: Company XYZ announced today that its earnings per share rose from $4.61 to $5.36 for the quarter ending June 30, 1982.

YES: Earnings up sharply at XYZ. For the just-ended quarter, they're up 75 cents a share . . .

When you try to cram too much information into your opening, the listener or viewer will be confused rather than enlightened. The soft lead can be a true public service, as well as an effective attention-getter.

NO: The Federal Government said today that there is insufficient scientific evidence to ban sodium nitrite, a commonly used food additive, as a cancer-causing agent.

YES: Sausage lovers won't have to give up their salami sandwiches yet. The Government said today there's not enough evidence . . .

ELIMINATE NONESSENTIALS   In journalism classes around the nation, students learn the standard "inverted pyramid" method of writing a news release; the most important facts are up front, followed by less significant details in descending order of importance.

Use a variation of the inverted pyramid for writing a news release broadcast style. Don't just delay those less significant details until the ninth or tenth paragraph. Eliminate them altogether. If the broadcaster must read your story in ninety seconds, he or she will only be able to read about 200 or 225 words. Why make that task more difficult by sending a 450-word news release?

Instead, take the initiative yourself. Make the hard decisions. What is truly important? What does the viewer or listener need to know? Think about it carefully, and then weed out those nonessentials. The busy broadcaster will surely be grateful, and your reward may well be an airing of your company or organization's news story on the local station.

WRITE SPARINGLY   Your first draft will nearly always be more wordy than necessary. Work over that draft until you have eliminated every nonessential word or phrase, cut out every redundancy, and bumped every flowery adjective, vague verb and pompous passage.

NO: His powerful speech was received with a standing ovation by the enthralled crowd of enthusiastic spectators.
YES: His speech won a standing ovation.

Watch for word-wasting phrases that can be shortened or eliminated without changing the meaning.

NO: At the present time, we can't afford it.
YES: We can't afford it now.

Here are some other phrases that waste space and don't contribute to meaning:

NO:	*YES:*
In the event of	If
In many cases	Often
In the majority of instances	Usually

Precision and clarity are your rewards when you take the time to edit and distill your writing. That's probably why every important handbook on writing will offer you similar advice. But there is one difference. Clean, sharp, spare writing is welcome everywhere. In broadcast, it is essential.

Write for the Ear

Broadcast style is conversational, not stiff or stilted. It's the language of friend talking to friend across the kitchen table.

USE SHORT WORDS Write in terms that are familiar to the average viewer or listener. *The Wall Street Journal* reports that although the average American recognizes about 20,000 of the 140,000 words in the general English vocabulary, the vocabulary of television contains only about 7,000 words.

NO: The energy required to reconstitute aluminum scrap is but a minimal fraction of that necessary to extract virgin metal from bauxite.

YES: Recycling aluminum requires only five percent of the energy used to produce it.

USE SHORT SIMPLE SENTENCES Remember, the viewers and listeners have only one chance to grasp what you are trying to say. If they get lost in the third modifier of that long, complex sentence, they can't go back and reread it as they would a *New York Times* lead. Instead, they'll probably just shrug and flip to another station or channel.

If your sentence seems to be getting too complicated, try breaking it down into two or more thoughts.

NO: The primary financial goal of the XYZ Company is to achieve the greatest possible return for our shareholders, maximizing the opportunity, and minimizing the risk.

YES: We want our shareholders to make money. That is XYZ Company's number one financial goal.

KEEP NUMBERS AND STATISTICS TO A MINIMUM   A newspaper article loaded with statistics may make illuminating reading; in a broadcast setting, those same statistics are just confusing. Pick and choose.

NO: Our national survey of 500 employed married women between the ages of 21 and 45 revealed that 18 percent prefer to shop for personal apparrel through catlogues, 72 percent would rather shop in stores and 10 percent had no preference.

YES: Career women still prefer to see it before they buy it. That's what 72 percent told researchers in a national poll.

USE QUOTATIONS WITH CAUTION   In print, a lively quote is an effective way to vary copy and make a point. In broadcast, that same quote can slow down the story, and sometimes be misinterpreted or misunderstood by the viewer or listener. Paraphrasing the speaker's statement is usually more clear.

NO: "It's our intention to provide the opportunity for a free and open exchange of ideas between employee and employer," chief negotiator Oscar Brown said.

YES: XYZ Company's chief negotiator, Oscar Brown, said the company wants to initiate better communication with employees.

Don't completely rule out quotes, however. A powerful quote can still add spark to a broadcast story. But to avoid misunderstanding, it's a good idea to write some kind of verbal lead-in to take the place of printed (and unseen) quotation marks.

NO: Board Chairman John Smith said, "The government agency, through its adversarial role, seems determined to increase its harrassment of business."

YES: Board Chairman John Smith challenged the government's adversarial stance. He charged the agency—in these words—"seems determined to increase its harrassment of business."

READ YOUR WRITING ALOUD   It's the best way to be aware of words or phrases that might be misunderstood by a listener, and to avoid such errors. The United Press broadcast stylebook offers a classic example of words that look one way and sound another. Reporting on a heavyweight fight, the announcer said, "The champion feinted a left." Listeners heard: "The champion fainted and left."

Tongue twisters and alliterations are other potential trouble spots. A string of words starting with the letter "s" will make the broadcaster sound like a whistling teapot. Also avoid indiscriminate use of personal pronouns. The listener, unlike the reader, cannot refer back to find out who is meant when the newscaster says "he found it hiding right in their own kitchen." Be sure every such reference is unmistakably clear.

Convey Action

As we have seen earlier, an important characteristic of the broadcast media is its immediacy. The viewer or listener is projected into the story, and becomes part of the action. Broadcast style projects that action and excitement. It uses clear, forceful language and active rather than passive verbs.

NO: The contract was ratified unanimously by the union membership.

YES: Union members unanimously approved the contract.

Radio and television are unique media. Their requirements are different from those of newspapers or magazines. The story that's written for print, with the old inverted pyramid formula and the five W's in the lead, just doesn't work for broadcast.

Rewrite your news release in broadcast style, and you'll see the difference in tangible results, specifically, more air time for the message of your company or organization.

WRITING THE QUERY LETTER

The most common form of written communication you'll have with a broadcaster is not the news release, but the "query letter."

You'll send a query letter (a story idea) whenever you have a suggestion for a broadcast story. It may suggest an in-studio interview with your company president on the firm's new expansion plans, or an on-location shoot of the rehearsal of the ballet your organization is sponsoring, or a feature on the exciting new volunteer program you've organized for youth in your community

You'll send a letter because most broadcasters prefer to receive ideas (except for late-breaking, hard news items) in writing. They are busy people with frequent deadlines and tough time pressures. Most don't have time for long phone conversations to explore the viability of an idea. They'll want to pick up your letter at their leisure, think through the broadcast possibilities of your proposal, formulate an approach and then quiz you on the details.

So, even when you call a broadcaster to sound out your idea, he or she will rarely make a commitment by phone. What you'll nearly always hear is: "Sounds interesting; send me something!"

That is your invitation to send a query letter. Whether invited or not, your letter is your primary sales tool, and the most important ambassador for your message or your story idea. It should be as strong, as forceful, and as convincing as you can possibly make it. Ideally then, your query should be written in broadcast style.

Too often, the techniques of broadcast style, acquired so painstakingly and with so much effort, are abandoned when the public relations practitioner sits down to write a letter. Those old, formal, grammar school guidelines come pouring out, and the query letter has all the excitement and punch of yesterday's bathwater.

NO: Dear _____

I am writing to interest you in our New Volun-Teen program, which offers neglected teens the opportunity to earn high school credits by volunteering after school in government-funded day care centers. There are so many heart-warming stories that could be told by your Channel 5 cameras . . .

YES: Dear _____

Joy! It's reflected in sixteen-year-old Jennifer's eyes as Bobby takes his first halting step. It's in Bobby's trusting toddler face

as he reaches for the outstretched hand of his "big sister."
Your Channel 5 cameras will capture this caring and concern
if you'll visit our new Volun-Teen program . . .

The first letter is dull, self-serving, and traditional. It doesn't
speak in human terms. It doesn't attract your eye. It doesn't
catch your ear. It doesn't tell the broadcast journalist what he
or she needs to know—how this story would work on the
program, how listeners or viewers would benefit from knowing
about the Volun-Teen program.

Your story must stand on the basis of its own merits, and
its own news value. Your letter should point out that value,
clearly, distinctly and from the top.

That's why broadcast style works so well in writing the
query letter. The broadcast journalist thinks in broadcast terms.
So, write that way. Convey vividly, not only the essence of your
idea, but how it would play on radio or television. The results
will be more effective broadcast opportunities for your company or organization.

Elements of a Broadcast Query Letter

Here are some basic guidelines for writing an effective broadcast query letter. If you think some sound familiar, congratu-
lations! You've been paying attention!

DISTILL   Find the essence. Summarize your topic in a
single word or a short phrase: "Old time religion!"; "Plastics!";
"Joy!"

Get the reader's attention. What is your subject? What are
you trying to convey? Find that word or phrase that best
describes the very essence of your idea. Start your letter there.

WRITE SPARINGLY   Pare your idea down to its briefest,
most meaningful essentials. Omit everything that is not intrinsic
to the story. "Don't tell me, sell me," advises one harried television producer. "Your letter should make me want to call you
and ask for more."

Here is a query letter that prompted a major network to send a camera crew thousands of miles. It worked because it was simple, sparse, clear, and told the recipient what she needed to know.

> Would the "XYZ Show" be interested in going to the Socialist Republic of Romania? Based on a conversation I just had with my Washington office, the Romanian government would welcome such a visit, and would cooperate with you and your staff in every way.
>
> Perhaps we can soon get together and discuss?

If you feel the broadcaster needs more than the barest information to make an informed judgement about your idea, don't incorporate all the facts into your letter. Supply them in supplementary form, with a news release (written broadcast style), a backgrounder or fact sheet, and perhaps a short biography or photo of the guest you're proposing.

KEEP IT SHORT   The ideal broadcast query letter is between six and ten sentences in length. It's *never* more than a page ("If it's long, I just won't read it," says a typical broadcast decision maker. "You can write four pages if you want to, but if you don't sell me in the first two paragraphs, forget it.")

THINK IN BROADCAST TERMS   If that radio or television journalist decides to pursue your idea, he or she will have to find a way to tell the story briefly, vividly, and succinctly. Show how it can be done by describing your idea in broadcast style. Don't expect the broadcaster to spend hours, or even precious minutes, studying and analyzing your three-page letter to find the angle that will make it an effective broadcast story.

USE A CONVERSATIONAL TONE   Remember short words and simple sentences. Convey your idea in an informal, colloquial tone, in the simplest possible language. This is the way the broadcaster will want to convey it on air. Eliminate the complex sentences, the technical language, the jargon, and statistics. If you can't tell your story easily and naturally in your letter, how can you expect the broadcaster to do so on radio or television?

TELL WHY YOUR IDEA IS VIABLE   Make clear in your letter that you are familiar with the format of the show you are targeting. Don't write in meaningless generalities. Don't say how "articulate" your spokesperson will be or how "moving" or "significant" your message is. Tell why and how your idea will fit the format of the particular show, and how and why it will interest that show's audience.

SEND YOUR LETTER TO THE RIGHT PERSON   It only takes a minute to call your local television station and make sure the person you think produces "Noon-Day News" is still in that job. A letter addressed to the right person (with the name spelled correctly) makes a better goodwill ambassador for your idea. Suggestions for finding the right person are discussed in Chapter Three.

Your query letter is the sales tool you rely on to market your idea. It needs impact; it must attract and hold attention. If you letter is written in broadcast style, it will have those qualities, and the recipient will quickly see the broadcast potential of your idea.

chapter six

Get-On Techniques

You need to develop a game plan if you want to take advantage of those many opportunities awaiting you in radio and television. You need a method for getting your suggestion read, your program idea considered, and your story told.

You need a game plan because competition for air time is ferocious. There's only a limited amount available. And there are so many who have good stories worth telling—government figures, charitable and nonprofit organizations, public pressure groups, celebrities, and business organizations, from the local doughnut shop to the Fortune 500 corporation.

How can you hold your own, and get your share in this highly competitive media marketplace? Creativity! If you are creative in "targeting" your story idea to the needs and demands of the media, you will have a success rate you and your organization will be proud of.

Following are some get-on techniques to increase your success ratio.

Creative Formatting

Do you know the three topics television and radio cover most often? They are health, sex, and money. That's really not so surprising, since these are the same topics we're most likely to talk with family or friends about over dinner or cocktails.

Maybe you think your story idea isn't related to health, sex or money. Think again! When you find a way to format your idea, to tie it into one of these subjects, you'll have a giant head start on your competition. Following is an example of how creative formatting works.

> A publisher of a well-known encyclopedia wanted major regional broadcast exposure. And if you think people at home shy away from encyclopedia salesmen, try getting one on radio or television!
>
> Creative formatting came to the rescue. A list of "questions everyone should ask a door-to-door salesman" was developed. (Sample: Where are you from?) along with some guidelines (If he's from out of town, beware). The questions and answers were so timely and useful that nearly every consumer broadcaster approached scheduled an interview. A creative consumer information segment had been formulated. The story had been tied to saving people money.

Creative formatting is simply coming up with a topical idea and an imaginative way to present it in order to capture the attention of the program producer or the talk show host and their audience. It's an especially useful technique when you have a story that's hard to sell, or when you're aiming at a national program that's unusually popular. As in the following situation:

> A national airline wanted publicity about new uniforms just designed for their flight attendants. Two problems: they wanted the story on a particular national entertainment program; and a few months earlier, the new designer-created uniforms of a competing airline had been widely publicized. (Those "Me Too" stories can be hard to place).
>
> The uniforms featured options. Each wearer could choose fashion boots or flats, scarves or capes, A-line dresses or aprons to achieve her own special look. Using that angle, a "game" was created for the talk show host.
>
> He would choose his favorite fashion options, and his choices would reveal his own personal "ideal woman."
>
> On air, attractive flight attendants modeled the new uniforms with optional accessories. The host, seated comfortably in a first class plane seat provided by the airline, deliberated between "swinger" (boots), conservative (apron, dress), traditional (A-line and flats), and so on.

When he announced his favorite, he was totally surprised when out from the wings came his "dream girl," one of the airlines' first stewardesses, dressed in her 1930 uniform! The host laughed. The audience roared. The airline was ecstatic. This creatively formatted segment was an enormous hit.

If you can creatively format your idea, and tie it to the hottest broadcast topics—health, sex, or money—you will be off to a good start in getting your story on air.

Talent Involvement

Often, feature broadcast reporters and talk show personalities not only want to "cover" a story, they want to "feel" it, and be a part of it. That's why the chance for your story to get on air will be greatly enhanced if you can factor in an opportunity to involve talent.

In the "ideal woman" game formatted for the airline, the television personality was an integral part of the segment. That's talent involvement. Here's another example:

A fiberglass manufacturer brought an exhibition to New York demonstrating ways fiberglass could be used in sporting equipment. The highlight was a battery-operated fiberglass golf cart which followed the golfer around the course. The golf cart proved a natural vehicle for talent involvement. Just about every television segment ended, predictably, showing the news reporter walking down New York's Fifth Avenue with the battery-powered golf cart trailing behind!

Enticing the reporter or talk show personality out of the studio and into an eye-catching setting or an unusual situation is a technique that will please both broadcaster and audience. One especially lively segment:

A home products manufacturer hired a very human-looking talking robot to demonstrate its latest products at a national trade show. The wise-cracking, guitar-playing robot was a hit among buyers at the show.

But a good television opportunity became even more terrific

when the company talked an attractive reporter from a local station into accompanying the robot on a "date." Cameras followed the two from the trade show booth to a cab ride through the city and on to a drink at a local cocktail lounge. Everybody had a great time!

If you're constantly aware of opportunities for hosts and hostesses to get involved with the story, you will improve your track record in broadcast placement.

Slicing a Story

As we've seen, it's important to know something about the focus or the format of the program you're aiming at before you try to place your idea. You'll have the best shot at getting on when your story fits the program's format.

That doesn't mean there's only one type of show that's suitable for your organization, or even for your story idea. What it *does* mean is that you need to pay attention to what aspect of your story will work for a particular audience or a particular format. Then "slice" your story to give it added dimension and extend it by focusing on a variety of angles that will make it work in a number of different programming formats.

Here's how one "education" story was sliced.

An aquatic chemist at a major chemical company developed a new ecology lesson plan for use by trade school teachers. The company donated copies to schools throughout its home state. The project was newsworthy (kids help) and it easily attained local coverage as an education feature, showing how it was used to teach ecology to youngsters in the classroom.

But slicing the story brought the same message to a wide number of broadcasting outlets. There was a wire-service-fed radio business feature describing how the lesson plan had sparked goodwill for the company; an interview with the chemist who had developed the program made a good science story, and a national TV segment was arranged when a popular network children's program featured the story on its kid's news segment.

In slicing your story, look beyond the obvious. Try to see what angles might appeal to the sports editor, the science editor, the consumer reporter, and even the weather person:

> A nonprofit organization planned a Sunday afternoon bike-a-thon. The project got publicity from virtually every local radio and television station when a volunteer called all the weather forecasters and asked them to incorporate the event in Saturday's report.
>
> Many did, and the sun shone brightly on a profitable afternoon.

Your success in slicing your story will play an important role in how many viewers and listeners you reach.

Thinking Seasonally

Holidays and seasons are good devices for getting broadcast publicity. Can you tie your organization or your product to summer, fall, winter, spring, back-to-school, or graduation? How about Easter, Christmas, July Fourth, Valentine's Day, Mothers' Day, Labor Day . . . or New Year's Eve:

> A bottle of imported champagne was featured in a delightful segment on a popular network talk show. The company suggested the host and hostess toast the New Year with a bottle of its own sparkling bubbly, and provided a gigantic bottle of the beverage just for the occasion.

Sometimes it can be worth delaying your story if you can foresee a strong seasonal tie-in down the road.

> A supplier of vitamins and minerals to turkey farmers assembled an intriguing slide presentation on the history of the turkey. The original intent was to send it in September to local television stations in the farm belt.
>
> Someone suggested the story be held just before Thanksgiving. The result: viewers of a widely-viewed network morning show saw segments from the presentation on Thanksgiving Day.

Broadcasters are always on the alert for good original material with a seasonal or holiday angle. Give them some help, and you may land some very valuable air time.

Working with Celebrities

Celebrities not only make news. They *are* news. When you are working with a name that's recognized, it's a given that you'll have an easier time placing your story. Radio and television producers like to light up their marquees with big names. It helps build audiences.

Celebrities help you, too, by giving extra impact to your story. But use caution. There needs to be a smooth and natural connection—a transition between the celebrity you've selected and the message he or she is to convey. Otherwise, your celebrity interview may happen, but your message will never be given, or just as disastrously will be edited out.

Here's how one company successfully integrated celebrity and story.

> A popular screen star agreed to serve as spokesperson for a firm that manufactured bedspreads and draperies. In her talk show appearances, she confided that she had always secretly yearned to be an interior designer. She brought slides showing some beautifully decorated homes of other stars and celebrities she knew. It was a simple matter to make the transition to the discussion of the manufacturer's draperies and spreads.

Here's another example of a strong natural tie-in between celebrity and topic.

> A trade association of tire vulcanizers (tire retreaders) wanted to promote the idea that it costs less, in terms of dollars and in terms of oil consumption, to retread a tire than to produce a new one. Additionally, retreaded tires have an environmental benefit, reducing the number of discarded tires marring our nation's landscape. The association retained an internationally prominent race car driver to serve as spokesperson for the environmental and economic advantages of vulcanized tires. The broadcast segments were effective because there was a natural marriage between celebrity and subject.

If you decide to hire a celebrity spokesperson, use caution and common sense. Don't just hire a celebrity because his or her name is familiar. Make sure there's a tie-in, and a good connection. Be wary of selecting someone who is currently in the headlines. Some celebrities are so much in demand, and so quotable, that their presence may well overshadow any message you hope to convey.

Knowing the Broadcaster's "Hot Buttons"

Public relations, especially broadcast media contact, is a "people" business. It's very personalized. If you take the time to get to know the people at your "target" broadcast program, and if you can get some insight into the kinds of stories that excite those decision makers, you'll be one up on your competition. Just knowing that a producer at a network show is an avid gardener or that a popular talk show host is "into" gourmet foods may be the reason for an important placement some day.

> A network news correspondent was a wine enthusiast to the point where he grew grapes in his own vineyard and made wine in a still in his basement. His interest in the subject of wines made it easier to attain network coverage of the introduction of a new wine product.

It's a lot easier to get an airing for your story when some decision maker has a built-in interest in your subject matter.

> A computer company developed a program that analyzed the movements of athletes to detect areas of physical weakness. The computer and the program were donated to the United States Olympic training facility where our athletes are prepared for world competition.
> The public relations professional for the company knew that a host of a network talk show was a dedicated jogger. The computer, the movement analysis program and the company all received some valuable coverage when the talk show personality, in jogging attire, was filmed running through Central Park. Later, in-studio, the computer analyzed the strengths and weaknesses of the host's jogging form before a national audience. Here, host involvement and knowing the "hot but-

tons" were both used to develop a meaningful network television spot.

Based on that segment. the company sold a major installation.

The same technique is just as effective as a means of reaching
your local radio and television broadcasters. Take the time to
learn their "hot buttons" and use that knowledge to interest
them in your story idea.

Using News to Make News

Your story idea is more likely to find a place in the flow of
material used by radio and television producers if you remain
aware of when and how it relates to the news of the day. If
that message is timely and relevant, broadcasters will be far
more inclined to pay attention and say, "Hey, that's a good
story!"

New or proposed laws on the local, state or national level
may help put your company in the spotlight, if they are relevant to your industry or your product. For example:

New federal legislation requiring food manufacturers to label
products with specific nutritional information made news. It
also created a media opportunity for a firm supplying vita-
mins and other nutrients to the food industry.

Many radio and television consumer programs were eager to
interview a company spokesperson who could clearly describe
how the new law worked and how it would benefit the average
American.

Using news to make news may require you to do a little "pack-
aging" and to think of your organization or your product in a
new way. If your competition is closing a plant in your town,
that news may create an interview opportunity for your company spokesperson to talk about all the many ways *your* firm
is benefiting the community and its people. Here's a way one
company put that philosophy to work.

It was rare to pick up a newspaper or watch a television business segment without reading or seeing another indication of

how Japanese manufacturers were burying American industry, especially in such key areas as automobile production and electronics. An American manufacturer of car stereo speakers used that news peg to schedule interviews for the company president with broadcast business and consumer reporters across the country. His message: Top of the line car speakers are produced not in Japan, but here in the United States, and business is booming. That angle, and ensuing guidelines on how to choose the right stereo equipment, created an effective use of air time for the company and the consumer.

If you develop a "nose for news" and stay alert to ways in which the news is relevant to your organization, you will find the welcome mat out at many broadcast studios.

Creating News

Perhaps your company or your organization doesn't have the remotest connection with the news of the day. Don't despair! Create your own news.

There are many proven techniques for creating a news story or a newsworthy event that will provide fine radio and television opportunities for your organization. Some are complex and large in scope, like the Virginia Slims' Tennis Tournament and The Colgate Women's Games.

Others are far less expensive, easier to arrange, and perhaps equally effective. When you begin to think about it, you may be surprised by how often your company or organization is creating news without even trying. When you begin to recognize those news-making situations, you will greatly expand your broadcast opportunities.

A *survey* or study, for example, is a common means of creating news, especially if the topic is either very timely (the most economical style of car on the market) or very off-beat (how many corporate presidents cook their own breakfasts). Most people are curious about the results of interesting or topical surveys, and so are most broadcasters. You will be able to generate a number of good interviews for your company spokesperson when your survey has been completed, provided of course it has yielded some notable or surprising results.

A food company wanted to publicize a nutritious new snack food being introduced on the marketplace. The company hired as spokesperson a well-known nutritionist who had studied the daily diets of team athletes at a major university.

Her five-year study identified some surprising differences in nutritional needs of athletes in different sports. The study was a natural springboard for radio and television interviews focusing on the snacking habits of Americans, and eventually on the snack food being promoted.

BOOKLETS AND BROCHURES are broadcast news generators, especially if your company is willing to provide them to the public at no cost. The vitamin supplier we described earlier developed a handy reference guidebook, describing how food labels can help plan more nutritious meals. So did the editors of the encyclopedia sold door-to-door. Broadcasters like the idea of being able to offer their viewers and listeners free consumer information. These booklets generated many broadcast interview opportunities for the company spokesperson.

ANNIVERSARIES can be the news peg to spark a broadcast segment featuring your company or organization. That's especially true if you can connect that anniversary with a strong human interest angle.

A manufacturer of elevators observed its 125th anniversary. The company's public relations department assembled a fascinating collection of photographs, historical data and statistical tidbits on "the world's safest vehicle," and supplied some great film of unusual elevators in action.

The company's anniversary was observed with coverage on two competing network morning programs—a rare feat for a feature story.

TRADE SHOWS OR CONVENTIONS can be effective means of making news in a community other than your own. When you or executives from your company or organization plan to attend an out-of-town affair, contact radio and television talk shows in that community. You'll probably be able to arrange one or more interviews to discuss the future of your industry, or new products and services available to the consumer.

Remember, though, that you won't be the only company coming to town during that trade show or convention. When those events occur, producers and assignment editors are often inundated with interview suggestions. So plan on an especially long "lead time" when proposing your idea. Contact the station four to six weeks prior to the show. Try to be the first in line for an interview opportunity.

AWARDS are another way to create news. A manufacturer of cameras might name outstanding photographers. A producer of building materials could recognize an architect who designed the most energy-efficient building. Perhaps your company or organization already recognizes an outstanding employee, a volunteer of the year, a special achievement or a money-saving idea. The recipient of your award will often make an effective spokesperson to represent the company or organization on air.

Spotting News Trends

There are fashions in news, just as there are new dress fashions each year. Several years ago, ecology was trendy. Then, stories on energy took center stage. Still later, it was "cope news"— ideas audiences could use to improve the quality of their lives, cope with inflation, government regulations, taxes, unemployment, and interest rates. The economy is always in vogue.

If you learn to identify fashions in news and you can relate your story idea to the current trend, you will often find broadcasters who are interested in featuring your message.

Using Visuals

When you think of television, think visuals. Television is pictures that move. Story ideas featuring only a "talking head" will generally lose out to the more eye-appealing competition.

If you bring broadcasters good story ideas backed up with interesting film or videotape, you will have a much improved chance of success. Companies or organizations often maintain a library of "file footage" that can be used to support and enhance their messages. A hospital might have visuals videotaped in the operating room. A utility company could create some interesting footage in the control room that is usually off limits to television camera crews.

> A communications conglomerate developed a technique to help visually impaired people send mailgrams in Braille. A national television science reporter liked the story and interviewed a company executive.
>
> A few days passed and the interview hadn't aired. A query yielded the reason; the producer thought the segment was "visually weak."
>
> The firm hired a cameraman to shoot some footage of the Braillegram computer in operation. The video was supplied and the segment ran.

Good visuals are often the missing ingredient that can help a newsworthy story get on air, or enhance a "talking head" interview with your organization's executive or spokesperson.

If you can't supply the visuals, be sure you do have a few good suggestions as to how the broadcaster can format your story idea with moving pictures.

> The manufacturer of a luxury car wanted to introduce its most expensive model on network television. The idea became reality when the company president offered to chauffeur the host of a popular morning program around New York's Central Park. Thus, a piece of "product publicity" was transformed into a visually delightful segment.

The get-on techniques described here are not new. They've been used successfully for years by highly paid public relations professionals in major metropolitan markets, and by savvy volunteers for cost conscious charitable organizations in every tiny village across America.

They've been listed here not because they're new, but because they work. Put them to work for you and your organization and experience the satisfaction of seeing your story told before the radio and television audiences of America.

chapter seven

Mounting A Media Tour

The media tour is a proven way to get meaningful exposure for your message in selected media markets. The tour is a series of short one- to three-day) visits to selected media markets (cities, regions) during which time your company or organization spokesperson is interviewed by radio, television, and print journalists.

The number and location of the cities (markets) you choose for your media tour depends on a number of factors: purpose, budget, and marketing strategy. You can choose as few as three or as many as three dozen markets. You can focus on the "major markets" (those ten or twelve cities in which the majority of our population is concentrated) or you can choose selected markets based on sales or fund raising goals, geographic location, media opportunities, convenience, or any number of other factors.

Does the media tour work? One company researched the question and now uses media tours as a routine marketing strategy.

A manufacturer of baking soda wanted to publicize the fact that its product was an effective water purifier for backyard swimming pools. The manufacturer was essentially a one-product company, depending on more sales of its only product for increased profit. The company decided to use the promotion of this additional use of baking soda to test the effectiveness of a media tour. In five cities, the firm mounted an advertising blitz. In five other cities, the same ad campaign was preceded by a media tour in which a spokesperson described on radio and television interviews how adding baking soda to one's home swimming pool would combat water problems specific to that community. Sales improved in all ten cities. But in the five cities where the media tour was conducted, the sales curve went off the page.

The media tour is cost effective. For a comparatively small investment, your company or organization can literally saturate a market with your message or viewpoint. The generally accepted media tour schedule calls for a minimum of two television interviews, three radio interviews and one print interview in each market. Compare that air time and print space with the amount you could purchase with ad dollars in those markets, and the cost effectiveness is readily apparent.

In addition, the media tour gives your message or viewpoint the advantage of an implied "third party endorsement." Ads are effective, but many Americans today react to them with a certain degree of skepticism. We all know anyone can buy time on radio or television to tell the world how great they are. On the other hand, when a neutral third party, a trusted broadcast journalist, talks about your idea or program or project in a news or feature editorial format, it attains a different kind of credibility.

Planning and coordinating a media tour is a specialized art form at many top public relations agencies. But the techniques are not mysterious secrets, known only by a privileged few. They are the very same techniques described throughout this book, but organized and structured to reach a specific goal.

By following the steps outlined here, you can plan and carry out a media tour that will be as successful as any organized by the most experienced specialist.

WHEN IS A MEDIA TOUR APPROPRIATE?

There are several sound reasons for deciding to mount a media tour. Let's examine a few of them.

Launch a Product

Organize a media tour to help launch a new product or service (as described earlier) or to encourage more use of the same.

> A toy manufacturer introduced an innovative new doll, which made soft cooing sounds when it was handled. Preceding a broad ad campaign, the company mounted a ten-city tour to major markets. The spokesperson, curator of a well-known museum, traced the history of dolls in America and showed examples of the most intriguing dolls of past eras. The last example in the presentation was the company's newest doll. The product was the hit of the holiday season that year.

A rule of thumb: For the greatest effectiveness, it's preferable to precede an advertising campaign with the public relations tour. After the ads start appearing, your story will not appear as newsworthy to editorial decision makers.

Express a Viewpoint

Schedule a media tour when you have a viewpoint you want to express on a current issue or when your company, product or service is in the news.

> A nationally known chemical company is in the forefront of discussion on the environmental issues which impact on the chemical industry—clean air, clean water, toxic waste disposal, and use of pesticides and herbicides. This company uses the media tour program as a routine means of scheduling knowledgeable representatives in key cities around the country to discuss the pros and cons of pending environmental legislation. Because the company spokespersons have legitimate credentials and are well-informed and ethical in their approach, the company has developed a reputation as a credible, reputable organization.

Broadcast journalists have not only an ethical, but a legal obligation to air contrasting views on controversial issues (see Chapter One). Therefore, if you can provide a credible spokesperson who can speak knowledgeably about current problems or controversies, you will often be able to secure meaningful air time for that person.

Image Enhancement

Plan a media tour to improve the public image of your company or organization, or to counteract problems your company or industry may be experiencing in specific geographic areas.

> A professional organization wanted to counteract the influence of "retail" medical outlets that were proliferating in some cities around the country. The organization used a media tour in which local members of the group were booked as guests on key talk shows to provide consumer information on how to choose and evaluate the best medical care. The consumer segments proved effective in enhancing the image of the medical profession.

Boost Sales

Try a media tour to boost sales of your product or service in specific markets or to build awareness of your product or service in areas that are most important to you.

> A prominent moving company compiled some comprehensive statistics on the number of families on the move and the cities most frequently moved to and from. The company then chose the most mobile areas and scheduled a spokesperson to provide consumer tips such as how to pack, choosing a mover, and how to get acquainted in a new city. Local media liked the segments because the information had a local orientation; viewers and listeners found them a source of valuable information.

Coordinate with Travel

Plan a media tour around the existing travel plans of your top executives or key spokespersons. This alternative is a good way to "test the waters" of the media tour format for your company or organization. You simply tie in media appearances as your executives travel around the country. If the head of your research lab plans to make a speech in Omaha, or your CEO is attending a seminar in Chicago, contact the local media in those cities and schedule an interview or two.

> The president of a company that produced stereo speakers agreed to schedule a few radio and television interviews in cities where he was visiting corporate sales offices. The interviews (described in Chapter Six) were so successful and attracted such enthusiastic responses from local retail outlets and from consumers that he now regularly plans such appearances to coordinate with his travel schedule.

The media tour, carefully planned and professionally executed, can be a very satisfying, very successful marketing and public relations tool for your company or organization.

PLANNING A MEDIA TOUR

Lead Time

Planning and coordinating a media tour means bringing together a host of small details. Coordination and careful planning are very important. You need to work well in advance; an effective tour is not just "thrown together" at the last minute.

The number and location of cities where you are scheduling your tour, the time of year, the potential impact of your message, and the kinds of radio and television programs you are targeting are all factors in determining the amount of lead time necessary.

A general rule of thumb is to allow a minimum of three to six weeks lead time. Add a week or two for major markets, or more if you are aiming for the very top talk shows in those markets. If your story has a strong current news hook, you can probably organize a very effective media tour in a much shorter period of time. The same can be said for a story format that features a top name celebrity or a top newsmaking personality.

If you truly have a "heavy-hitter" as a spokesperson, the rule of several weeks lead time is less critical.

Many of the most popular talk shows book guests as much as two or three months in advance of the air date. On the other hand, every show experiences last minute changes and cancellations. Don't hesitate to contact a top show even if you suspect the dates your spokesperson is available may be filled. There is a chance, often a good chance, that there will be time available for an interesting spokesperson with a well-presented topic . . . *your* spokesperson and *your* topic.

Markets

Selection of the cities where you'll send your spokesperson is very often a marketing decision. Ask yourself, or your marketing department: Where do we want to sell our product? Where do we want to be better known? Where is our company or our industry experiencing problems that we want to counteract?

The most popular cities for media tours are generally those with the greatest population concentration. New York, Los Angeles, Chicago, San Francisco, Philadelphia, Detroit, Boston, Washington, Houston, and Dallas usually appear among the top ten markets on most industry rankings. (You can get up-to-date annual rankings of market size from 1-100 from such trade publications as *Advertising Age* and such industry resources as *Broadcasting Yearbook*). Just keep in mind that the larger the market, the greater the competition for air time and the harder you will have to work to schedule interviews for your spokesperson.

Besides marketing strategy and size of population, another criterion for experienced tour planners is media opportunity. So-called "joint markets," where two large metropolitan areas are contiguous or close enough together to make intercity travel practical, will offer two sets of media to draw upon in scheduling your spokesperson. Examples include such areas as Baltimore/Washington, Minneapolis/St. Paul, Seattle/Tacoma, Dallas/Fort Worth, and Tampa/St. Petersburg. Other examples are available in those same trade publications and resource books.

In planning your tour, be aware of logistics and organize accordingly. Don't have your spokesperson hopping from coast to coast, or flying thousands of miles with just a short stop in each city. A well-planned tour might begin in Boston, then travel to New York, Philadelphia, Washington, Atlanta, Miami . . . and so on. Schedule two cities per week, three at the outside. Leave time for travel and occasional days of rest and recuperation for your spokesperson.

The Right Time

Time of year can be very important to the success of your media tour. Select a month or a season in which your message is most timely and interesting. The story about nutritious Halloween treats that radio and television talk shows snapped up in September and October will be tough to book in the cold winds of November and December. A graduation story will lose its impact quickly after the diplomas have been handed out and classrooms are locked up for the summer.

> A manufacturer of housewares and paper products wanted to beef up sales of its paper towels. A how-to segment was formatted showing how a variety of Easter decorations could be made from the paper product. The company spokesperson visited a dozen cities in the weeks just prior to Easter, and the tour was a creative and marketing success.

Be aware of special dates that will create either unusual difficulties or special opportunities for your spokesperson. Generally, weekends are not good times for booking talk show appearances. On the other hand, it may be easier to get air time on an evening news program on a Saturday or a Sunday than it is on weekdays. Be aware of periods when the networks conduct their regular ratings sweeps, in November, February, and April. That's when every local station makes an extra effort to schedule blockbuster guests and celebrities who will attract large number of viewers. It's an ideal time to come through with a celebrity spokesperson. If you don't have one, don't expect as much high-visibility air time as you would have at other times.

Localize the Idea

Just as you need to come up with a "get-on" device to obtain air time in your own community, you need a creative format for your media tour. You can use any or all of the techniques described in Chapter Six to format your idea. But there's one cardinal rule to keep in mind above all others when formatting a media tour, and that is to localize your story. Identify a local angle, a regional tie-in. Ask yourself: Why would a producer in St. Louis, Portland, or Denver, be interested in booking my spokesperson as a guest on his or her show?

> A camera manufacturer planned a media tour to introduce its newest type of camera. The spokesperson was an artist-turned-photographer, who used the camera as an innovative tool in creating unusual works of art. In each city, the photographer displayed his technique by photographing local landmarks (the Golden Gate Bridge, Times Square, the Washington Monument) and incorporating those scenes into his artistic creations. The idea was enthusiastically received from coast to coast.

The more creative you can be in providing a local angle for your media tour, the more air time you will achieve. Following is another example of a localized approach.

> A prominent manufacturer of small computers mounted a media tour designed to show the versatility and the "human" applications of its product. The company identified users in cities across the country who were applying its computer in innovative ways. In each city, broadcasters were offered a "smorgasbord" of local applications of the computer, with a representative of the company on hand to explain how computers are invaluable aids for science, education, administration of justice, and scores of other areas. The result: a variety of broadcast interviews in each community, each showcasing a different computer application.

The computer company example illustrates another essential of formatting for a media tour. Although you will have one basic format, be flexible enough to vary the theme to meet the needs of a variety of programs. Your media tour will be most successful if you can adapt your format to a variety of programming needs, from in-studio talk show interviews to on-location news segments, and from radio call-in programs to debates.

Spokesperson

Once you've decided upon your format, the choice of a spokesperson will become less difficult. If you are embarking on an issue oriented tour, you will want an individual with sound credentials who is extremely well-informed on the topic to be discussed. If your goal is to improve your company image in cities where your major plants are located, or where you have large retail outlets, you may want to schedule a high ranking, articulate executive of your company or organization. For topics of a consumer nature, choose an expert who will arouse the interest and curiosity of the editorial decision maker and broadcast audience.

> A company was introducing a new heavy-duty, stretchable fabric to be used for making luggage. The spokesperson chosen for a multimarket media tour was the author of a best selling travel book. Her topic: How to pack a versatile wardrobe for a month in Europe in just one suitcase. The author and her informative demonstration were snapped up by television talk shows across the country.

Few local broadcast producers are interested in booking "visiting firemen" just because they happen to be passing through town. Your spokesperson needs sound credentials, expertise or a name that arouses public interest. If you want to talk about a new food product, try to find a great chef, or someone who's written a best selling cookbook, or a celebrity with a reputation for culinary skill. Don't get your plant manager or the supervisor of your own test kitchen. Look for neutral third parties, preferably with some kind of name recognition, like authors, editors of trade books, academics, or artists. If your spokesperson is obviously a representative of your organization's front office, expect some skepticism on the part of the media.

Sometimes, imagination and creativity are fine substitutes for hiring a celebrity spokesperson. The key is to find a person with sound credentials, and who will attract and keep the attention of the broadcaster and the broadcast audience.

A company that produced home safety systems hired a former burglar who had served time for breaking and entering. The spokesperson offered a fascinating inside look at his "profession," and some timely tips on how consumers could protect their homes from unwelcome intruders. The media tour was a total success.

Preparing Your Spokesperson

Not every spokesperson you choose will be expert in the realities of radio and television interviews. It's part of your job to make sure the person you choose is well-prepared before he or she embarks on the media tour.

First, make sure your spokesperson knows the topic thoroughly. An articulate spokesperson will provide what the broadcasters have every right to expect—information that is accurate and fresh and presented in an interesting and authoritative manner.

Brief your spokesperson on any negative questions that may arise during the interview. It is necessary to know how to carefully and credibly incorporate your company or organization's name into each and every interview. If the person does not have previous broadcast experience, it's a good idea to expose him or her to some simulated interviews that are videotaped and played back, to demonstrate visually how the spokesperson will look and sound in an actual interview situation. (More tips on preparing a spokesperson in Chapter Nine.)

Budget

The budget you have available to you will have a significant impact on your media tour plans, the number and location of markets you choose, and the person you select as spokesperson.

Budgets can fluctuate widely, but here are basic media tour expenses you will probably need to include in your calculations:

- Hiring and/or training spokesperson
- Preparation of written materials and any needed visuals
- Mail and phone costs of contacting media
- Travel expenses for spokesperson (possibly for someone to accompany spokesperson)
- Hotels and meals on the road
- Cost of air checks (tapes of aired segments)
- Your time (or time of person organizing the tour)

CONTACTING THE MEDIA

Choosing the Right Shows

When you're booking a media tour in a market hundreds of miles from your office, you won't have the opportunity to meet and get to know the decision makers at each station. You can't watch or listen to all the potential shows in order to decide which ones are right for you. You have to rely on your contact books (see Chapter Three) and other industry resources, your own experience, your own good judgement, and your own common sense.

But there are some guidelines you can use to zero in on the shows that will provide the best opportunities for your company or organization's message. Pay special attention to these criteria when you choose the programs you'll be contacting.

AUDIENCE SIZE   Go where the audiences are. Generally, stations with network affiliations will have the largest and most loyal audiences. Choose VHF over UHF television stations. For radio, check your contact books for the station's reach and power.

Audience Type Identify the audience you are after. Who are the people you want to reach? What shows are they probably watching or hearing? Develop a "media plan" as an advertiser would. Find out the names of the most popular shows for your target audience, and go after those first.

Air Time The time of day when a show airs helps determine the size and the make-up of the program's audience. Try to schedule your spokesperson at the most appropriate time of day for your message—a business story for afternoon drive time or evening news, a consumer segment for an early morning or noon-day talk show.

Program Format Talk shows are the bread and butter of most media tours. They generally book guests well in advance and, except in rare cases, their schedules are not subject to sudden cancellations. News, on the other hand, provides a high visibility format for your message, but the downside is that news assignment editors generally won't make a commitment until the very last moment, and even that commitment may be broken if a major news story breaks on the day your spokesperson is to appear. Media tour specialists generally plan schedules around popular talk shows, leaving time to schedule news interviews if the opportunity presents itself at the last minute.

Finding the Right Person

Once you have decided which stations and programs you want to contact, you need to determine a contact person at that station. When you're working with unfamiliar media in faraway cities, you need to rely heavily on the contact books in your library. Be sure your resource materials are up-to-date.

If you haven't made recent contacts in a market, choose the top four or five shows you have selected and make some phone calls. Find out who books the guest interviews at each station in which you're interested. If you can, talk up your idea while you're on the line. Sometimes the editor's initial reaction can give you some valuable feedback in making final formatting plans for your message.

But whatever you do, *get a name*. Try never to send a letter without being sure you are addressing it to the right person, the person who is the producer, the talent, or the assignment editor at the station.

Sending Written Materials

Whether or not you've spoken to the decision maker at your target program, you'll need to send some written materials before most stations will make a commitment to schedule your spokesperson.

As in all written materials prepared for the broadcast journalist, the media tour materials should be clear, concise, and convincing. The most successful package for a media tour will include a *short* query letter (not more than a page), describing your idea and how it would be formatted to fit the individual program, a *short* background piece (not more than a page and a half), and perhaps a brief biography and a photo of your spokesperson. And that's all! Here is one example of where less is more. The heavier the package you mail out, the less likely your chances of getting your spokesperson on air. (For tips on preparing written materials, see Chapter Five.)

Scheduling Interviews

A week to ten days after sending your written materials, follow-up by phone. Talk with the decision maker to whom you sent the material to ascertain interest and to arrange an interview.

In assembling a media tour schedule within an individual market, pay attention to the logistics and details. To arrange a feasible schedule, be sure you learn the answers to these questions:

- Where will the interview take place? (In-studio, on-location.) Get exact address.

- What time should the guest appear at the station or interview location?
- What time will the interview begin?
- What is the expected length of the interview?
- Will it be taped or live?
- Will the spokesperson be alone or with someone else? If someone else, who?
- What is the name of the program on which it will air?
- What is the anticipated air date/air time? (if taped)
- Who will conduct the interview at the station?
- What is the name and telephone number of the station contact person who scheduled the interview?
- What is the format of the interview? What is the topic?
- What visuals or props should the spokesperson have on hand?

Note answers to all these questions on a schedule (see Figure One for sample schedule). Send one copy of the completed schedule to the spokesperson and keep one copy in your office.

Common sense and an eye for detail are your most important allies in arranging the logistics of a media tour. Plan the time of your spokesperson so he or she is neither rushing from place to place nor sitting idle for hours between interviews.

In planning the schedule, consider not only the time consumed at each interview, but travel time and distance between points. If your spokesperson is in unfamiliar territory or if your tour is in a major metropolitan area, add extra travel time. Allow for contingencies.

Be sure to provide time for your spokesperson to eat breakfast, lunch and dinner and take an occasional breather. Probably if you plan more than four interviews in a single day, you are overextending your spokesperson.

A word about exclusivity: Few programs will ask for an exclusive, except for major shows in the largest markets. Unless it is requested, don't offer an exclusive. When you are faced with such a request, make sure the station, program, and format are worth this concession. Don't make this decision lightly.

Producers of two high visibility shows in a major west coast city insisted on an assurance of exclusivity before they would schedule an interview with a spokeswoman for a large moving company. Faced with an either-or decision, the public relations professional chose the program with the largest audience. It turned out to be a poor choice. The producer of the rejected program had been enthusiastic about the interview and would have alloted several minutes to the topic. The hostess of the selected program was indifferent, lethargic, and uncooperative in allowing the spokeswoman to communicate her message.

Size and type of audience, the enthusiasm of the producer for your idea, and the prestige of the program are all factors to be weighed when you must decide on exclusivity. It can take the wisdom of Solomon.

Confirming Interview Arrangements

Get into the habit of writing a short letter confirming time, date and topic with each program as soon as you hang up the phone after making the arrangements. Keep a copy for your own records.

Telephone confirmations of every interview should be made routinely a day in advance of the interview date.

FOLLOWING A TOUR

A professional follow-up procedure will go a long way toward making your media tour an effective public relations vehicle for your company or organization.

Start by writing thank-you notes to the broadcasters with whom you scheduled interviews. This is a courteous gesture that takes little time and is well worth the effort. Express your gratitude for the broadcasters' interest in talking to your spokesperson. Tell them you look forward to working with them again on future stories of mutual interest. Be sincere and professional.

If budget permits, engage a monitoring service to video-tape or audiotape the interviews when they air. These "air checks" help you to see firsthand how your message has been integrated into the station's programming. It's both enlightening for you and impressive for your company or organization executives.

Besides collecting air checks, keep a record and compile a comprehensive report of the interviews scheduled in each city, the station on which they appeared, the minutes of air time, and the audience size. This information will help convey the effectiveness of the media tour to your marketing people.

chapter eight

Producing Your Own
Broadcast Materials

Self-produced broadcast materials! There's a fertile, but little-explored market in both radio and television for the audio and video materials you produce independently, providing they are timely, newsworthy, not overly commercial or self-serving and of professional technical and editorial quality.

Throughout this text, we've described ways to motivate local broadcasters to include your story or message in their programming. But there is another alternative, one too often overlooked by public relations professionals.

Producing and distributing your own radio or television news and feature stories, whether in very brief, abbreviated segments or full-length formats, presents an increasingly attractive option in your broadcast media relations planning. Today, thanks to the explosion of distribution sources for radio, television and new technologies, the variety and reach of outlets for self-produced broadcast materials has never been greater.

You can contact local radio and television stations in your own community and in other areas where your company or organization has a presence. You can work with public access and commercial lease channels at your local cable system. You can syndicate your programming via existing radio and television news and programming services. You can work with national radio and television networks, and with production houses serving national cable networks, both pay and ad sponsored channels. You can even create your own ad hoc network of commercial stations and/or cable channels, distributing your material via satellite for down-link to those broadcasters who choose to air it.

ADVANTAGES OF SELF-PRODUCED MATERIALS

Self-produced materials, distributed to broadcasters via telephone, audio or videocassette or by satellite, offer some distinct advantages in a public relations program for your company or organization.

Control

You have editorial control over the content of self-produced material. Because you are the producer, you decide who will be interviewed, what points will be stressed, and what will be eliminated or edited from the final version. You can tell your story exactly the way you want it told, so it will accomplish what you want accomplished. If you're seeking to enhance your organization's visibility, your name and your logo will be an integral part of the story line. If you're selling a product, listeners or viewers will hear the name of the product, or see that product in action. If you have a viewpoint to convey, your spokespeople will have the opportunity to put across your copy points clearly and effectively.

Cost Effectiveness

Costs of producing and distributing audio or video far exceed the expense of writing and sending a traditional printed news release. In many instances, though, they can be extremely cost effective methods for you and the broadcaster to reach listeners and viewers. For example, if you can most effectively convey your story via an interview with the chief executive officer of your company, use of an audio or video segment will save precious hours of that executive's time. One single interview can be taped, then distributed to broadcast stations in target cities across the country for airing on the evening news. If your story requires on-location shots of your facilities, you can provide those visuals to local stations far distant from your plant or your office, stations that lack the budget or staff to send camera crews to you.

Compared with advertising, self-produced audio and video materials are far less costly; because they offer that all-important "third party endorsement" that comes with editorial exposure on news and information programs, they have a credibility that advertising can rarely achieve.

Versatility

Self-produced broadcast materials, especially video, are extremely versatile. The footage you take in the process of producing a video news feature, for example, can be edited and used in a variety of ways—for employee communications, as a marketing tool, for analyst presentations or new business proposals. You can tuck the material under the arm of your spokesperson as he or she travels the country on a media tour, and incorporate it into the speeches of your company executives. You can use it for staff or volunteer recruitment, or as the centerpiece of a fund raising campaign.

Possibilities for other uses of self-produced audio and video materials are limited only by your creativity.

Prestige

Producing high quality broadcast materials can enhance your reputation with the broadcast community. When your products meet or exceed high professional standards, you are showing broadcasters that you understand them and their language. Soon you will be seen as an alternative source of legitimate programming.

TYPES OF PRODUCTIONS

Self-produced materials can run the gamut, from a thirty-second audiotape "voice actuality," phone-fed to radio stations across the country, to a ninety minute, star-studded television special underwritten by your company or organization. Your budget, the broadcast media you select for distribution, and most of all, your communications objective, determine the scope and the type of production you will undertake.

Here is a sampling of the diverse formats that lend themselves to self-produced broadcast segments.

Short Radio Formats

Radio segments of thirty, sixty or ninety seconds, which can be integrated easily into the news and information programming of local stations, are the least costly to produce and often the most popular with broadcasters, especially when they are newsworthy and/or have a message of interest to local listeners or viewers.

You can distribute a thirty- or forty-five-second audiocassette with the most up-to-date news about your company or organization to local broadcast stations across the country. Record a statement from your chairman describing the new production method developed by your research department and telling how it will reduce the cost of your product and create more jobs in your plants. If you have plants or retail outlets in twenty cities across the country, it's a good bet that broadcasters in those cities will happily accept and air your material in some form.

For radio, there are two widely used methods of distribution: mail and telephone feed. Many people opt to send their radio materials on cassettes through the mail. The disadvantage here, and it's a significant one, is that a tape arriving in the mail lacks the timeliness and urgency of the "same day" delivery you can achieve on the phone. A mailed cassette says to the

broadcaster, "This really isn't news; it can keep for a day or a week or forever!"

On the other hand, a phone-fed taped actuality conveys a message of importance and urgency. It says: "This is hot, this is something that can't wait." In most cases, phone-fed audio materials will get a far more enthusiastic reception from radio decision makers. You are providing local news told in the voice of your company chairman. If you make that material available while the news is still fresh and timely, and if the audio material you provide is of professional broadcast quality, your self-produced news report will find a place in the news flow of many local stations, stations that would not have had the facilities or staff to get that story themselves.

> The nation's first domestic communications satellite was introduced to radio audiences coast-to-coast via a series of audio phone feeds produced by the developing firm. The first feed, preceded by a lead-in describing the significance of the event, was a taped recording of the inaugural message transmitted by satellite—a statement from the mayor of New York to the mayor of Los Angeles. Other audio segments followed as uses of the satellite were expanded. The newsworthy segments were widely used by stations coast-to-coast.

A good, solid self-produced radio segment with a well-known spokesperson and a timely message can sometimes achieve the same results as an effective broadcast commercial, at a fraction of the cost.

Short audio segments can also be effective ways for your company or organization to respond instantaneously and effectively to a crisis, while still using management time efficiently.

Imagine, for example, that your company has been indicted by the Environmental Protection Agency for alleged violation of clean air standards. The story is being broadcast on the morning drive time news. You produce a tape of your company chairman or another key spokesperson, stating very briefly, clearly, and directly the company response to the report.

Within a few hours or even less, you can telephone twenty, fifty or 100 radio news departments, feeding that same audiotape over and over again to broadcasters in communities where the allegations are of interest, offering to provide your response in the interest of fair and balanced reporting. Many of those stations will accept and air your response because it is timely and it offers balance and authenticity, a reality that simply does not come through via a printed news release.

Organizations that have timely news or information reports to offer on a regular basis can use a self-produced audio-cassette and a toll-free number to make those reports available to broadcast stations with minimal cost and effort for either party.

> A major automobile manufacturer assembled a daily business report focusing on up-to-date news in its industry. A former broadcast business news reporter was hired to tape the report each day, and the company actively promoted the service to broadcasters throughout the country. Many radio news departments called the toll-free number daily, recorded the message as it played, and aired the reports on morning and afternoon drive times.

If you decide to establish this kind of service, it's not enough to simply have it. You need to promote it on a continuous basis. Call key stations regularly. Send letters. Remind broadcasters of the service. Point out highlights of the kind of materials you're providing. Advertise in trade journals that are read by broadcasters. Offer useful information and keep talking it up. You will find a steady stream of users.

Some public relations professionals prefer to format multi-part series to showcase their companies or organizations in more than one segment. These are especially effective when your story has a feature orientation.

> A major producer of automobile polishes and waxes sponsored an international road racing event featuring top name drivers. The company aligned an ad hoc network of several dozen stations and phone-fed three race reports: a prerace feature, a midrace update, and a postrace segment. Each report incorporated the company name—an effective promotional tool for its automotive car products.

Multipart series, both audio and video, are popular with many broadcasters because they provide the continuity, consistency, and audience interest of a mini-documentary. A relevant, topical, informative series produced by you will be welcomed in the newsrooms of many local broadcast stations, because it will keep the audience coming back for more. You are making available, free of charge, quality material that many radio stations have neither the staff nor the budget to produce.

In addition to distribution to individual local stations, short audio segments or multipart series that are of national interest can be offered to radio networks or to national news, feature, or programming services.

Long Radio Formats

Less common than short actualities and features, but still highly do-able and very effective, are self-produced radio programs of thirty or sixty minutes or even longer. To produce and place these full-length productions requires a substantial budget, careful advance research (is there a market for your idea?) and a very salable approach. You'll be competing for air time with hundreds of other program suppliers, many of them professionals with years of experience: radio networks, news services, wire services, syndicates and production houses. Your material must be first-rate, top of the line.

On the plus side, more and more of the thousands of local radio stations on air today are moving to a news and information format. Hampered by skeleton staffs and shrinking profits, many are trying to compete for radio audiences with large, well-financed stations. These smaller stations are viable markets for professionally produced, well-conceived programming that will attract, entertain, and enlighten their audiences.

A national soft drink bottler wanted to reach the young people who were primary buyers of the product. A ninety-minute radio production on the history of rock and roll, narrated by a popular disk jockey and featuring "Golden Oldie" sound tracks, was formulated and made available to radio stations. The production was an enormous hit with broadcasters and teens.

This production was successful because it effectively met the specialized needs of the broadcasters who aired it. It offered high quality, audience-grabbing programming that many local stations lacked budget and staff to produce themselves. This ninety-minute production had the added benefit of versatility. Broadcasters could divide it and air it in several parts, or offer two forty-five-minute or one ninety-minute program. Shortened versions, sound bites from the longer piece, could be edited out and used as fillers throughout the day or week.

The long radio format can also be ideal for a public affairs program produced and distributed by a nonprofit organization.

Short Television Formats

Local television stations, especially smaller stations or those in secondary or tertiary markets, provide ample opportunities for professionally produced video news and feature materials distributed on cassette tapes or via satellite.

Sometimes, self-produced visuals are supplied by companies or organizations to supplement and support a news release or an announcement of some type. New product demonstrations on video, distributed to local stations with a news release and/or a suggested script, are a common example. Even these very simple productions must meet professional television standards if they are to be aired by quality-conscious broadcasters.

A manufacturer introduced its new microwave oven with a self-produced news clip demonstrating how the oven could fry a slice of bacon in less than a minute. The piece got the cold shoulder from every television station, even though the product was revolutionary at the time.

When queried, producers were unanimous in their responses.

Watching bacon fry, they said, wasn't much better than watching a still picture. The segment lacked visual interest; thus, it was of no interest to television stations.

Television, like radio, demands that material produced by outside sources be of professional technical and editorial quality, be free of self-serving, overt commercialism and offer timely, useful information to viewers. Additionally, to work on television, your material must have a strong visual angle. As said earlier, the essence of good television is moving pictures. Without strong visual interest, your self-produced video material will probably not be aired.

More and more local television stations, even smaller ones, now have satellite receiving capabilities. Thanks to satellite transmission, companies and organizations can now offer local stations around the country self-produced audio and video actualities of newsmaking events on the day they take place. Highlights of your news conference in San Antonio, for example, can be transmitted via satellite to stations thousands of miles distant. Provided your event made news of interest to local viewers in Atlanta and Portland and Milwaukee, many stations in those cities and others might be interested in incorporating your materials into their local newscasts or including them in a more in depth news feature examining a related subject.

Complete self-produced video news feature segments, in sixty or ninety-second formats, can be highly efficient and effective vehicles for your message to reach the millions of upscale, educated viewers who tune in to local news broadcasts each evening.

Consider a self-produced video news feature when:

- Your story has broad news or feature appeal—it can be tied to a national news event, issue or trend. or be localized to appeal to viewers in widely scattered geographic areas.
- Your story can be portrayed visually with interesting pictures that move.
- It would be difficult for local broadcasters to produce the story independently.

- You have or can hire professional equipment and television production expertise.
- You want to retain editorial and technical control over the final product.

> The manufacturer of a mini-computer wrote software that transformed its computer into a reading machine for the blind. The computer translated printed words into audible messages. The manufacturer was confident this breakthrough would merit wide television coverage. What was less certain was whether a news segment initiated by broadcasters would include the brand name of the computer.
>
> The solution: A self-produced vido feature identifying the computer by name, which has been seen by over ten million viewers.

When your video news feature is "evergreen" (of interest over a long period of time) like the computerized reading machine for the blind, its cost effectiveness may be enhanced because of its long viewing life. Stations aired that particular tape months after it was first distributed.

On the other hand, there are definite advantages to self-produced materials tied to specific dates or current events of national significance. In those instances, stations will have an impetus for airing your material immediately, and it will be easier for you to track the number of stations which picked it up and the number of viewers exposed to your story.

> The government of a neighboring nation wanted Americans to know that country's engineers had designed and built the remote arm manipulator installed on NASA space shuttle flights beginning in the spring of 1982.
>
> A video news feature, in the form of a three-part series, was produced and distributed to American television stations just a few weeks before the launch of Columbia II. The series described how the remote arm was developed and how it would contribute to scientific research in space. Almost 100 network affiliates and independent stations aired the multipart series during prime time news in the weeks prior to the launch, reaching an estimated audience of over six million viewers.

This subject was ideal for a self-produced video news feature. It was timely, newsworthy, exciting, visually appealing, and tied to a pending national event of interest to nearly every

American. Further, the visuals so intrinsic to the story—shots of the space arm in development and in action—were not easily available to camera crews of most local stations. The self-produced materials provided these stations with valuable information they could not have obtained on their own.

Multipart segments can be designed to air on consecutive days, like the space shuttle series. Another viable alternative is producing a larger number of short feature segments and syndicating them to broadcasters as weekly "mini-features." You can syndicate by approaching national broadcast services (see Chapter Two) or by contacting local stations individually.

> A national nonprofit organization serving young people in trouble produced an eighteen-part series of ninety-second interviews with a family psychologist. Each segment offered advice on a problem area of concern to parents—how to deal with an adolescent runaway, how to predict a potential teenage suicide. The entire series was made available free of charge to local stations around the country; many aired this thoughtful approach to parent-child relationships as a viewer service on highly visible daytime talk shows.

The key to success in this series, like any self-produced video material, was top quality production and editorial standards, absence of overt commercialism and a topical idea that grabbed the attention and the interest of broadcast producers.

When you can put together those basic essentials, your story may be an ideal prospect for a self-produced audio or video segment or series.

Long Television Formats

In the early days of television, major advertisers (some of the nation's largest corporations) made their names household words by underwriting the full cost of weekly, highly visible network television shows—The Colgate Comedy Hour, Kraft Music Hall, Philco Theater, United States Steel Hour.

Until very recently, we thought those days were gone. With skyrocketing costs of network television advertising, even the largest companies confined their television spending to a few thirty-second ad spots on prime time network sit-coms or sports events. At most, the largest and most public-spirited have underwritten a one-time special on public broadcast or an occasional network documentary.

Today, with the explosion of local cable systems and national cable networks, the pendulum is swinging back in the other direction. Both locally and nationally, public relations-conscious companies and organizations are again finding it economically viable to produce or to underwrite the production costs of full-length television programs, now on cable. Many are experimenting with new approaches made possible by new technology, teletext, videotex, Qube, and satellite linkages.

> A franchise offering travel packages put together a series of "infomercials," seven- to ten-minute segments with a talk show format discussing topics of interest to travelers—how to choose a travel agent, how to decide which Caribbean Island is right for you. The segments aired on an experimental interactive Qube system, and viewers could indicate interest in getting more information by pressing a button in their own homes. The infomercials proved very effective. The local agency experienced the lowest cost per sale of any of that company's franchises.

Opportunities for self-produced, full-length programming exist today in a wide variety of cable outlets. Many of the nation's largest advertisers are again underwriting costs of weekly programs, this time targeted to specific demographic audiences and aired on ad supported cable networks. A food wholesaler sponsors a weekly cable program focusing on women who are outstanding achievers. A manufacturer of childcare products underwrites a weekly cable program on parent-child relationships.

The same approach is being taken on a smaller scale by local companies with good ideas but more limited budgets. These forward-looking firms are taking advantage of local cable access channels to reach target audiences with self-produced "life management" information and other timely news and feature material.

> A savings and loan association in the midwest produced an eighteen-part series offering personal finance advice to viewers.

The business editor of the local newspaper was hired as host, and the series was aired on the local cable public access channel, reaching thousands of viewers in that metropolitan area.

In the east, another financial institution had a similar idea and met with similar success. In this case, the bank collaborated with a well-known accounting firm to produce four thirty-minute programs offering tax tips and strategies to consumers. The programs aired every three months at key time periods, on the commercial lease channels in the area, reaching thousands of households.

On commercial television, opportunities to air your self-produced full-length segments may be more limited, but they still are available in some markets, particularly in weekend daytime slots that are sometimes reserved for public affairs-type programming.

A major oil company produced a series of "energy update" videotapes designed to offer background information to broadcast journalists during the height of the energy crisis. Because the tapes were so timely and so professionally done, many stations decided to air them in a thirty-minute program for viewers as a public service.

Federal regulations require broadcast stations to identify the source of information when accepting and airing materials produced by outside sources. Therefore, you can't expect your full-length, self-produced materials, however professional, to be accepted by the commercial networks or by the biggest commercial stations in major markets. But many others (enough to make this technique cost effective) will consider them provided they meet the high broadcast standards described earlier.

PRODUCTION GUIDELINES

Production of broadcast-ready radio and television material is a very viable and effective part of the full range of broadcast public relations possibilities. But embarking on an in-house broadcast production usually requires a substantial investment of time and money. Such projects should not be undertaken lightly.

Have a Game Plan

Before you begin production, get a firm idea of how you'll format and position your idea. Here are some questions to ask yourself before you get underway.

- What is your communications objective? (What story or message do you want to convey?)
- What is your target audience?
- What medium—radio, commercial television, cable—will you target?
- If television or cable, what visuals will you use to tell the story?
- What length production will fulfill your needs?
- How will you format or position your story to make it air-worthy in your target markets?
- Will it fly?

Sample the Market

Once your production goals and plans are clear, call some producers at four or five key stations in markets where you'd like to see your materials aired. Describe your idea. Ask whether they would consider airing the production when it's completed. Ask how the message might be better targeted to their needs. At the same time you are gauging interest in your idea, you may get some help from the pros that will help you better position your story or message.

If your advance research indicates there's little enthusiasm for your project, don't discount that information. Go back to the drawing board. Reassess your idea. Don't make a major investment of money or time until you're sure there is a market for your final project.

Use Professional Talent and Equipment

You can't tape even a thirty-second product demo with a home eight-millimeter camera and expect broadcasters to accept it. To do the job properly, you need top quality, professional equipment; the same kind used by broadcast studios. You need to work with videotape, not film, because that's what is being used in television today.

Similarly, you can't cut corners by using unskilled or inexperienced talent to produce your broadcast materials. The people you hire—writer, field producer, camera crew, audio or video technician—must have broadcast experience. That's especially important when working with television materials. A filmmaker, even a very good one, may not know television. It's a very different medium in its pacing and its use of visuals. Film experience may not provide these sensitivities.

Broadcast experience is just as important when you choose the talent, whether voice-over or on air. Use former radio or television personalities, or moonlighters for professional results.

Hearing or seeing material you produced yourself on radio or television is a satisfaction available to very few people. The growing number of outlets for high quality, self-produced broadcast materials will make that satisfaction attainable for more and more public relations professionals in the years ahead.

part three

THE
HOW
FOR THE EXECUTIVE

chapter nine

Effective
Broadcast Interviews

The broadcast interview! Ideally, it's a way to converse informally and naturally with the people you want to reach. Used wisely, it's a modern alternative to the face-to-face, friendly relationships that existed in the past between the neighborhood business and its customers, the town's favorite charitable organization and its donors.

An interview on radio and television is an opportunity for you to communicate meaningfully, personally, and effectively. In effect, you are chatting individually with the viewer or listener while he or she is sitting comfortably on the living room sofa. That's why broadcast interviews can be so effective in helping your company or organization make warm, personal, human contacts with the public.

Unfortunately, business and industry executives, along with representatives of nonprofit organizations often fail to use broadcast interviews to full advantage. Instead, too many squander precious air time with weak, ineffectual performances. They're passive, defensive, apprehensive—and it shows. They fail to convey a sense of credibility and authority. Their interviews are not believable.

It's one thing to be accorded air time to represent your company or organization on radio or television. It's another to use that air time effectively and efficiently, and to communicate your message clearly, concisely, convincingly.

Here are some guidelines to the *attitudes* you need and *techniques* you can use in every broadcast interview.

ATTITUDE

Don't Be Passive

All too often, executives who would *never* appear at a Board of Directors meeting without a carefully planned presentation backed up by a thirty-page report, will arrive at a broadcast interview with only the most casual notion of what they plan to say.

The naive executive sits down across from the interviewer and waits expectantly for that open-ended question that will open the door for the story he or she wants to tell: "Tell me, what brings you here today?" or "Won't you tell us all about the new product your company is introducing next week?"

Of course, in most cases, the broadcast interviewer doesn't cooperate. The "logical" question—the one that leads right to your message—is never asked. Before you know it, the interview is over, and you never had a chance to say the things you wanted to say. You waited for the hanging curve, but it was never pitched.

It happens all the time. But it doesn't have to be that way. You don't have to sit back in your chair in the broadcast studio and hope the right questions will be asked. You can seize the initiative, and take control. You can make every broadcast interview an opportunity to communicate what *you* want to communicate.

> The chief executive of a public utility was invited to be interviewed on a live radio talk show. Because of a conflict in schedules, the executive declined, but sent a qualified spokesperson to speak for the company. The interview began on a hostile note. "Why was the chief executive not available? Was he afraid to speak on such touchy subjects as rate increases or nuclear power?" the reporter wanted to know.
>
> The substitute spokesperson made a valiant effort to answer the questions, to explain her boss would have been available at any other time. But the reporter was tenacious and kept up the same line of questioning. "Look," the young woman finally said, "you can keep asking me questions like this and we won't accomplish anything. Or you can ask me some ques-

tions that are of interest to your listeners." The direction of the interview shifted rapidly, and the reporter addressed his subject with new respect.

This woman knew the importance of taking the initiative, of getting off the defensive. She successfully took control of a potentially disastrous interview and steered it into productive territory.

Henry Kissinger was a master at the art of controlling an interview—and he knew it. His famous opening line at a morning news conference reveals that confidence: "Does any reporter have any questions for my answers?"

Mr. Kissinger was able to control interviews because he was prepared. He was preprogrammed to make every meeting with the news media an opportunity to say what *he* wanted to say. He knew reporters were not there to serve him. It was his job to take the initiative—to seize control. One Hall of Fame broadcaster once described this technique as "answering the question that wasn't asked."

Don't Be Defensive

The very nature of the broadcast interview may tend to put the guest on the defensive. It's like a one-sided tennis match. The interviewer serves a question, the guest returns an answer. As long as the reporter keeps serving questions, the guest is on the defensive, because, as tennis buffs know, the server always has the advantage. If you just sit back, receiving those questions and responding, you'll never wrest the advantage away from the interviewer. He or she will have you running to and fro, backing you into one corner, then another. Finally, you'll lose the point, the game, and the match.

So, get off the defensive. Make every question work for you. Wrest the advantage away from the interviewer. Don't just answer questions, but *use* those questions as opportunities to talk about the things *you* came to say. Initiate topics of your own. The burden is on you, not the interviewer, to make sure the listener or viewer gets the message you came to convey.

Show Your Enthusiasm

You ought to view every broadcast interview as a sales call. It's an opportunity for you to get your foot in the door, grab the viewer or listener by the lapels, and sell your product, idea, or organization.

You need enthusiasm to sell your story. If you look or sound apathetic, as though you don't really care much about what you're saying, the audience won't care either. If you're bored, the audience will be bored. If you can't project some excitement into your presentation, you may as well just send a printed news release and say you can't make it that day.

In the effective interview, you'll convey a sense of your own enthusiasm, and a sense of excitement and urgency about your topic. You won't just offer facts and opinions. You'll tell why those facts and opinions matter to you, and why they should matter to your audience.

TECHNIQUES

You're on the right track when you approach every broadcast interview with an upbeat attitude, determined not to be passive or defensive, determined to project enthusiasm and excitement, and prepared to create your own opportunities by initiating topic ideas of your own. Now you need to master the techniques to translate that attitude into results.

Interview techniques focus on three areas: preparation, cosmetics, and on-air strategies. All are equally important.

Preparation: You Need a Game Plan

It's essential to approach every broadcast interview with a game plan in mind. Preparation is the key to control. Control is the key to an effective interview. To prepare, you must:

PREVIEW THE PROGRAM   It's important to know as much as you can about the format of the program on which your interview will air. Know the kind of audience likely to be tuned in, and the approach of the broadcaster who will interview you. Watch or listen to the program as often as you can. Look for answers to questions like these:

- Will the interview be taped or live?
- What time of day does the program air?
- How long are most guests on air—thirty seconds, three minutes or a half-hour?
- What kind of people are probably watching or listening?
- Does the show accept questions from the audience?
- Do guests appear one at a time or are they members of a panel? If part of a panel, who are the other panelists? Are they friendly or unfriendly?
- Is the interviewer friendly to guests, or antagonistic?
- Is the tone of the program informational, confrontational, entertaining?

Too often, spokespeople agree to an interview without asking these key questions.

A brief telephone conversation with the program's host or producer can be productive too. Ask what general subjects will be covered in the interview so you can be adequately prepared. Ask about the approximate length of your interview, and what other people will be interviewed on the same topic. For television, ask if visuals would be helpful and arrange to bring slides, charts, graphs, or best of all, videotapes or film.

CHOOSE THE RIGHT SPOKESPERSON   You have the right and the obligation to choose who will speak for your company or organization on air. The format of the interview, the audience and the subject matter help decide who is the right spokesperson for the particular interview.

Often, the chief executive of your company or organization is the best choice. The days of the executive hiding behind closed doors or sending canned statements to the media are long gone. When company or organizational policy is on the line, the audience wants and expects to see the top authority.

Your company or organziation needs that individual out front, speaking up, telling your story openly and honestly.

But the top person isn't always the right person. Think in terms of qualification, ability to communicate, and credibility, rather than rank. The most appropriate spokesperson for a broadcast interview is the person who is most knowledgeable on the topic to be discussed. Be sure that person has the ability and/or training to communicate easily, clearly and effectively, and that he or she has no distracting visual features that will keep the viewers from concentrating on the message.

When the interview will focus on a new technological development in your research lab, the head of research and development at your company may be the best spokesperson. If you're talking about the annual marathon race your company is sponsoring in the community, choose the staff person organizing the event, or perhaps, an employee who competed last year.

KNOW YOUR OBJECTIVE   What is the purpose of your broadcast interview? What do you want viewers or listeners to take away from your appearance? What do you want to say?

An essential step in preparing for any broadcast interview is to closely examine those questions. Identify your communications objective. Decide in advance on the one or two key points (sometimes called "copy points") you want to convey to the listener or viewer.

In most broadcast situations, your communications objective should be limited to one (two at the most) because of the transient and compressed nature of the media. Radio and television deal with experience and impressions, not education or deep background. The audience of a broadcast interview has just one chance to hear you and absorb your message. You're on—then you're gone. There's no instant replay—no chance for the audience to go back and rehear what you've said. If you try to convey too much information in that condensed time period, your hearers or viewers will probably just get confused and tune out, mentally or actually. In either case, your interview opportunity will be wasted.

Make your communications objective as clear and specific and memorable as it can be:

POOR: XYZ Company is a good neighbor.
BETTER: XYZ Company is concerned about protecting the environment.
EFFECTIVE: XYZ Company voluntarily spent $5 million last year on a program to clean the Hudson River, making us a good neighbor concerned about protecting our environment.

ANTICIPATE QUESTIONS   If you are knowledgeable about your company or organization, and if you are aware of events and situations in the news that affect your field or industry, then you should never be surprised by a question addressed to you in a broadcast interview.

To avoid surprise, anticipate in advance the questions most likely to surface in your interview. Put yourself in the shoes of the broadcast interviewer. Pretend you are Mike Wallace or Barbara Walters, about to interview *you* concerning your company or organization. Prepare a long, detailed, comprehensive list of every question that might be asked in such an interview. Make them timely. Make them tough. Enlist the help of a knowledgeable colleague to make sure you've covered all the possible territory, especially any potentially negative questions.

In your preparation, don't just think about the obvious questions that logically relate to your company, your product, or your service. More often than not, your interviewer will come up with at least one "zinger"—an off-the-wall question that has only an incidental connection to you or your company or your organization. Perhaps you represent a bank, and there's been a recent scandal involving an executive at a major financial institution who was caught absconding with company funds. What will you say if you're asked how your bank would handle a similar situation?

Prepare for those zingers as well as the expected questions —the illogical as well as the logical. Usually, such questions will grow out of the headlines. Be aware of events in the news of the day that have some impact or some relationship, however nebulous, to your company, product, or service. That awareness will help you anticipate even surprise questions.

Think about how you might answer hypothetical questions: "What would you do if your company were facing an unfriendly acquisition as the ABC Company is?" (Your best response to a hypothetical question is a candid refusal to speculate. Don't conjecture. Talk about what you know. Say "I don't know what would happen if . . . Let me tell you what *is* happening.")

PLAN YOUR RESPONSES   When your list of questions is as complete as you can make it, review each one and decide how you want to answer it in the broadcast interview situation. Here are some special techniques to keep in mind as you plan your responses.

CRYSTALLIZE   Radio and television are condensed media, headline services. A broadcast interview is hardly ever the time for an in-depth exploration of your topic. A long, thoughtful statement stands a good chance of being either edited out or interrupted. Learn to crystallize your responses into short "sound bites" between twenty and forty seconds, and you will convey the crisp, authoritative image you seek, and that broadcast requires. As an added benefit, your comments will be less vulnerable to editing if the interview is being taped for airing at a later time.

BRIDGE FROM NEGATIVE TO POSITIVE   Be especially aware of areas that may be sensitive, and where there are negative perceptions you hope to turn around. With planning, you can build positive answers to negative questions by using those questions as bridges to your communications objectives.

Here's how one corporate executive successfully bridged from negative to positive in a nationally televised interview.

> The board chairman of a major chemical company was asked by a television interviewer whether criticism from environmentalists had caused his firm to stop manufacturing a controversial chemical (a negative and potentially loaded question). The executive responded with a candid "No," and explained

that manufacture of the chemical was stopped only after the company lost its contract bid. But he did not stop there. He continued his answer by pointing out that inasmuch as the chemical was no longer produced by his company, he thought it pointless to waste time discussing it. Then he went on to say, "But let me tell you about the products we *do* make," and described lifesaving vaccines and drugs the firm had developed.

Some call it "bridging." Some call it "transitioning." Whatever you call it, you should learn this simple, effective three-step technique. First, respond directly to the negative question ("No, the only reason we stopped producing the chemical was because we lost the government contract"). Then, continue with a brief transition statement ("But since we no longer make that product, let me tell you about something we *do* make"). Finally, introduce the topic you want to discuss, your communications objective ("We're proud of the new vaccines and drugs developed in our own research laboratories which are saving thousands of lives every year in underprivileged African nations").

When planning such responses, you may want to use the "15-10-15 Formula" to make sure those responses are concise and succinct. Time your direct response to about fifteen seconds, your transitioning statement to five or ten seconds, and your positive conclusion to about fifteen seconds. That way, your response will not exceed the forty- or forty-five-second time period that is usually most effective in a broadcast setting.

END ON A POSITIVE NOTE   This technique is sometimes known as "getting around the edit." That's not quite accurate because the guidelines here are not an exact science. They're geared to work, but they're not guaranteed to work. In the end, the decision of what should be aired and what should be eliminated is totally in the hands of the broadcast decision maker.

With that said, it is helpful to know that when your interview is being taped, most broadcasters don't like to edit statements in midsentence. It's difficult to air just part of a sentence without having it sound as though something is missing. Thus, when you're asked to respond to a negative question, answer directly, and then transition to a positive note. Complete every negative comment with a statement that is positive and favorable to you. That way, your negative reply will be balanced by a positive conclusion, and more than likely aired intact—just the way you said it.

> A New York City radio show focused on the city's contro- versial West Side Highway, which had fallen into disrepair. The broadcaster placed most of the blame for this disaster at the feet of former city planners.
>
> After stating his opinion that poor planning was the cause, the broadcaster inserted a taped "response" from one of the most prominent of the city planners. Heard on the air were these seven words: "That's crap, that's a lot of crap."

It's safe to assume that in compiling his story, the radio per- sonality had spoken to the planner at some length, long enough at least, to elicit more than these seven words. Yet this was the portion of the interview the broadcaster chose to excise, and these were the only words of response radio listeners heard.

There's no *guarantee* that this same kind of editing won't happen to you. You *can* make it much less likely, though, by capping any negative statement you make with a positive con- clusion.

Had the city planner completed his response by saying something like "That's a lot of nonsense because back in 1931, I personally recommended to the mayor that we not use cheap, inferior materials to build the highway," the entire sentence would probably have hit air.

Broadcast editors rarely cut a speaker's comment in mid- sentence. Knowing that can help you guard against unfair editing.

REHEARSE OUT LOUD   The final step in your preparation for the broadcast interview is practice. Have someone you trust —your son or daughter, wife or husband, secretary or colleague —ask you every question on your list. Practice answering each question until you're confident you can respond effectively and convincingly to each and every one.

In preparing for a broadcast interview, it's important to conduct this "rehearsal" out loud, especially if you lack broadcast experience. That way, each question and its most effective response will be filed away in your "mind's ear" and will come quickly to mind in the interview situation.

ARRIVE EARLY   It's a good idea to get to the broadcast studio ten or fifteen minutes early. Walk around. Ask questions. Familiarize yourself with the sights and sounds of the studio. Try to talk to someone—the receptionist, a member of the crew, the producer or the person who will interview you. Use the time to review your thoughts and your copy points. Check your image in a mirror or, better yet, the floor monitor to make sure your hair is combed and your jacket is buttoned correctly.

Cosmetics: Look as Good as You Sound

It's natural to be a little nervous as the day of your first broadcast interview arrives. In fact, a certain amount of nervousness is healthy and positive. It sharpens your senses, heightens your awareness, and puts you on mental alert.

So allow yourself to be a little nervous, but don't let it get out of hand. You want to be sensitized, not immobilized. Remember, this is a great opportunity to sell your ideas and convey your message.

DRESS APPROPRIATELY   On television, how you look is just as important as what you say. The clothing you choose should be conservative, not distracting. Don't let what you're wearing get in the way of what you're saying. Choose lightweight clothing that fits well and that you feel comfortable in.

For men, a suit in a dark solid tone is a better choice than a loud plaid; a suit is preferable to a sports jacket. Wear a long-sleeved shirt with about an inch of linen showing at the cuffs. Ties should be muted in tone, socks knee-length. Unless you're overly portly, keep your jacket buttoned. A buttoned suit jacket communicates order and control. It conveys to the viewer that you're on top of things.

For women, an attractive business suit or a conservative dress in a solid color will convey that same sense of authority and control. Avoid flashy jewelry and spiked heels. Women should wear their usual makeup, applied subtly. Men may want to apply a little neutral facial talcum powder to absorb moisture on the "hot spots"—the bridge of the nose, the forehead, the cheekbones, over the eyes.

Your clothing should not only be comfortable; it should inspire confidence and convey a sense of authority and believability. If you're wrinkled and disheveled, or carelessly groomed, you won't command attention and respect for your message from the television audience.

Sɪᴛ ɪɴ ᴛʜᴇ Exᴇᴄᴜᴛɪᴠᴇ Poꜱᴇ   From the first camera angle focusing on you, the television audience will be forming a mental image. You want to look as confident and authoritative as you sound. The audience should get a favorable impression of you even if there's an audio failure and they can't hear a word you say.

Adopt the executive pose—the comfortable and confident posture that shows you are in control of the situation. Cross your legs at the knee, not at the thigh or ankle. Fold hands one over the other (not clasped) and place them on your lap. Use your hands freely for any natural gestures. If you're seated on a chair with armrests, you can rest your elbows on them. But that's as relaxed as you should allow yourself to be. Don't lean back in that big, soft chair. Lean forward slightly, in the "attack" position. This posture keeps you alert and helps you concentrate. Above all, it says "confidence" and communicates self-assurance.

Watch your body language throughout the interview. Shifting in your seat implies you're uncomfortable with the question. A quick glance away from the interviewer before your response suggests reluctance to look the audience in the eye and weakens credibility. Folding your arms across your chest conveys the impression that you're combative or perhaps holding something back. Avoid nervous mannerisms—tapping your foot, wringing your hands. You never know where that camera is pointing.

ASSERT YOURSELF   The camera can be a friend or a foe. Camera angles can flatter or they can distort. Distances convey a sense of authority, or weakness. Network personalities are often shot very "tight" (up close) to give them more authority and credibility. Conversely, an unflattering angle or a close-up shot of your hands twitching or your feet tapping as you respond to a sensitive question may convey the image of an apprehensive, insincere, untrustworthy individual.

The camera is an important tool, but one you can influence when you're aware of its impact. Develop that awareness, then assert yourself. If you're extremely short, and you think your lack of stature won't convey the image you desire, ask in advance that the cameras concentrate on head and shoulder shots. That way, your image will fill up the screen and the audience won't be aware of your diminutive size.

DON'T BE INTIMIDATED   Once you've been seated and the interview is underway, refuse to be distracted or intimidated by the unfamiliar sights and sounds.

There will be floor managers throwing cues. Cameras will be moving from place to place. And perhaps most distracting of all, your interviewer may stop paying attention to you. While you're in midsentence, he or she will be looking at notes, anticipating the next question, consulting the clock to check the time before the next commercial break.

Don't let all that throw you. Keep right on talking. Look your interviewer in the eye, even if he or she isn't looking at you.

Don't look at the camera, unless you're specifically instructed to do so. Directing your remarks into the camera undermines your credibility by making you look *too* programmed, and *too* prepared. American audiences are conditioned to accept television as an "eavesdropping" medium. They're aware that when Diane Sawyer interviews the President, they are "listening in" on a conversation.

So maintain eye contact with the person who is interviewing you. Don't look down; that conveys a defensive, fearful attitude. Don't look up; that makes you look as though you're praying for divine guidance. Don't look away. Focus your gaze on the person you're talking to, eyeball to eyeball. It's a conversation. Ignore the cameras.

IN STUDIO

If you can only bring one thing with you to a broadcast interview, bring concentration. Once that interview is underway, thrust aside all distractions and focus your total attention on the interview process.

You need every ounce of concentration you possess to zero in on the questions, to weed out those parts that are unclear or unnecessary, to seize upon those parts that can be used to make your point and to make every word of every answer clear, forthright, and believable.

Here are some points to keep in mind once the interviewer directs that first question at you.

ANSWER DIRECTLY   The best response is a direct response. You want your interview to convey the image of a forthright, honest, sincere individual. You want to be believed. Begin by answering questions with a simple, declarative statement: "Yes;" "No;" "That's true;" "That's not true." Then add the embellishment.

This approach shows you are a sincere, candid person who does not evade issues or duck questions. It has another benefit. It puts you on track, points your answer in the targeted direction of your elaboration or explanation. Once you've responded with a direct "yes" or "no," the rest of your answer is likely to be relevant, not rambling.

Avoid the preface phrases some executives use almost automatically to hedge their bets. Say "No," not "I don't think so." Such prefaces are obscure, and they waste precious broadcast seconds.

Don't forget to bridge from that direct response to your

communications objective when appropriate, and to end negative statements on a positive note.

HUMANIZE YOURSELF AND YOUR COMPANY OR ORGANIZATION   You are not on air to speak for a structure of bricks and mortar, a balance sheet or a profit and loss statement. Your company or organization is a group of people, working together to create a product or a service of value.

Relate your message to the audience. What does it mean to the listener or viewer that your company produces the items it does, or that your organization provides its services to the community? Relate your message in personal, human terms. Don't talk about saving 30,000 barrels of oil. Talk in terms of an extra three tanks of gasoline for the car of every viewer or listener.

Radio and television are very personal media. They're wonderful for telling stories and anecdotes. So talk about your subject in human terms. Tell stories. Relate anecdotes. Humor can be a wonderful humanizer, if you're careful not to let your humor hurt someone else. Perhaps the best form of humor is poking fun at yourself. If you're the butt of the joke, you know your humor won't injure an innocent party.

In anecdotes and stories, strive to convey a feeling of warmth and humanity, to "people-ize" your company or organization. This is an especially important point for nonprofit and service organizations to remember. Too often, their campaigns and media appearances are so geared to numbers and dollar-oriented goals, that they seem to forget they're in the "people business." When the bottom line of everything you do is helping *people*, don't just talk numbers and dollars. Talk about the services those dollars buy. Tell about the people whose lives are better because of your organization. Talk about the many others who still need your help.

SMILE   A smile can say as much as a long, polite sentence, and say it better. When you open the interview by saying "Thank you very much for asking me to be on your program; I really appreciate the opportunity to tell your audience something about the XYZ Company," you've wasted ten precious seconds of air time. Amenities count for little in a broadcast interview. Few will be impressed by your good manners.

Instead, quickly get to the essence of your thoughts. Don't waste words. Say your "thank you" with a smile. Look comfortable and relaxed, as though you're happy to be there. Don't take yourself too seriously.

USE NAMES   Your credibility and believability will be enhanced if you take a page from the book of the late Egyptian Prime Minister Anwar El-Sadat, whose skill in conducting the warm and human interview greatly increased the prestige of his office and successfuly promoted the viewpoint of his people and his nation.

Why were Mr. Sadat's televised interviews so believable? One reason was his success in identifying himself as a friend of the interviewer in the minds of the audience. He accomplished this identification by the skillful use of first names—by calling Barbara Walters "Barbara" and Walter Cronkite "Walter." This subtle recognition of the interviewer as a person creates the image of a warm, caring, courteous individual. There's a suggestion that the interviewer and the guest are friends.

In contrast, addressing your interviewer by his or her surname may suggest coldness or stiffness. When you maintain that aloof formality, you may create in the minds of the audience an artificial barrier between you and the broadcast personality.

Use your own best judgement in applying this suggestion to the specific case. If in doubt, you might ask the reporter or host before the interview begins: "Would you mind if I called you by your first name?"

Sometimes you may see a public figure throw a casual arm across the shoulder of the interviewer, or touch his or her arm or knee. These can also be effective techniques to bridge the gap between you and the interviewer. Of course, don't overdo these techniques. Using the reporter's name more than once or twice will sound obvious or gratuitous. Gestures or body contact in the wrong situation will appear inappropriate or worse, presumptuous.

KNOW YOUR SUBJECT   It goes without saying that you should know your subject thoroughly. Do some homework before you turn up for a broadcast interview. Be able to support a statement with facts, especially if that statement is potentially controversial. But keep numbers and statistics to a minimum—one or two key statistics may be enlightening; more than that will merely confuse a broadcast audience. And don't get too detailed or too graphic in describing the unpleasant. No need to relate every possible side effect of the chemical you once produced at your plant. Simply say: "As soon as we learned it was a possible cause of cancer, we stopped production."

Be prepared, but don't pretend to know everything. Speak about what you know. If you're asked a question you can't answer, say so and offer to follow-up with the answer at a later date. Or better yet, be able to paraphrase what other experts have to say on the subject, while pointing out that your own expertise is in another area.

If you don't understand the interviewer's question, don't try to muddle through. Ask for a clarification before you respond. It's appropriate to ask for clarification when you need it. But don't ever answer a question with a question. Don't ask your interviewer what he or she would do if faced with your problem. It can get you into trouble. You are the expert. Don't evade that responsibility by asking questions of your interviewer.

BE INFORMAL AND CONVERSATIONAL   Use short words and simple sentences. Speak conversationally, as though you were talking to a friend over the dinner table or describing your family vacation to a co-worker. Talk with the interviewer the way you would talk to someone you like. Strive for an air of informality and naturalness. It's best not to bring a script or even written notes. If you're early on in your broadcast experience and feel you may need a crutch, you can carry notes on 3 x 5 cards. But try not to use them. Don't read.

If you come from a technical background, make a special effort to avoid jargon that will be incomprehensible to the average viewer or listener. If you must explain your technical process, choose the simplest possible language, as though you were talking to a third grade science class. Don't talk about effluent, talk about industrial waste.

Analogies can be a very effective way to simplify and clarify a complex issue, and to get your story told.

> An antinuclear referendum was on the ballot in a midwestern state, and a spokesperson from a manufacturer of nuclear power generating equipment toured the state, expounding on the advantages of nuclear energy. Invariably, the interviewer would ask the inevitable question. "What would happen to our community if that power plant were to blow up?" The response was a classic analogy: "Dick, the odds of that happening are the same as the odds that you and I will be hit by a meteor as we leave the studio tonight." The speaker's simple analogy helped defuse a major concern.

BE CONFIDENT   You know more about your company or organization, its history, its people, and the issues it faces than the reporter or the interviewer who is questioning you. You know more than the people who are watching or listening to you.

You are involved in that business or organization eight, ten or twelve hours every day. You are being interviewed because you are the expert. Your knowledge is your strength. Speak from that strength and you will succeed in broadcast interview situations.

DEALING WITH HOSTILE SITUATIONS

Any radio or television interview can be a harrowing experience, especially to the uninitiated. The lights, cameras, and microphones often create enormous pressure for those who aren't experienced in speaking on air.

With preparation, concentration, the right attitude, and by employing the proven techniques we've discussed, you will emerge from that defensive position, wrest the advantage away from the interviewer, and get your points across. Almost always. There are exceptions.

There are some broadcast journalists who take delight in baiting their guests by trying to get them emotionally involved. These are not simply reporters asking tough questions. If you're appearing on a broadcast interview, you ought to anticipate some tough questions, and be prepared to deal with them.

The broadcaster to beware of is the one, thankfully in the minority, who is openly biased, flagrantly slanted, or hopelessly antagonistic. His or her primary goal doesn't seem to be "getting a story." Instead, it's "watching you squirm."

If you are preparing for a radio or television interview with a hostile reporter, don't despair. These interviewers fall into some distinct, predictable categories, and there are tested, proven techniques for dealing with them.

The Machine Gun

The Machine Gun is the interviewer who asks you multipoint questions—so many you don't know which to answer first. "Why is your company intent on polluting our rivers? Why aren't you hiring (or promoting) more minority employees? How many women are on your board of directors? Why are your prices going up so fast? Don't you care about the plight of consumers?"

It's human nature to try to perform well. Your natural inclination will be to tackle it, and try to answer all the questions.

Don't! Instead, choose the *one* question you are most comfortable with, or that you can use to make the transition to your communications objective. Answer that one. Then let the reporter ask another question. It's a lot easier if you take them one at a time.

If none of the questions seem especially advantageous to you, remember that you are not obliged to answer *any* of the Machine Gun's questions. Instead, you can toss the ball back into the interviewer's court: "Well now, Bill, you've asked me several questions. Which one would you like me to answer first?"

The Interrupter

The Interrupter is the interviewer who never lets you complete a thought. This hostile interviewer asks a complex or provocative question, and waits until you're well into a productive, thoughtful answer, then he or she chimes in with a new thought or question.

If you follow the Interrupter's lead, you'll lose control of the interview. You'll never get back to completing the important thought you were developing. The interview will move on to a new topic, the conversation flow will drift away from you, and you won't have the chance to make your point.

You have two choices when dealing with an Interrupter. You can stop, listen patiently to the new question and suggest that you'll address that topic in a moment. Then continue your interrupted response with, "As I was saying . . ."

Or you can ignore the interruption, complete your thought and then address the interviewer: "Now, Sally, you asked me something else. What was it again?"

In either case, keep the initiative. Retain control. Stick with what you were saying. A new topic introduced before you've finished dealing with the first one will derail you from your course. The conversation flow will drift away from you, and you probably won't ever convey the key points you planned to make.

The pace of an interview is something you *can* control, even when you are being harangued by a hostile interviewer. When an Interrupter is bombarding you and peppering you with questions, don't allow the pace to accelerate by following his or her lead. Instead, regain control of the pace by taking a long pause, a five-second beat. Then respond in a very controlled, deliberate manner. If you're interrupted again, repeat with another long pause. Broadcasters hate "dead air." The interviewer will soon get the message. You will have reestablished a reasonable pace, and you'll be in control.

The Paraphraser

The Paraphraser is the antagonistic interviewer who unfairly and incorrectly restates everything you say: "In other words, you're suggesting that your company is distributing an unsafe product."

It's tempting to get angry and lose control in such a situation. But that's a mistake. Avoid getting emotional. Patience is the only effective weapon against a Paraphraser. Restate your position very carefully: "Fred, I guess I didn't make myself very clear. What I said was . . ." and then go through the whole scenario again, as clearly and crisply and concisely as you can.

It is essential that you take the initiative and demonstrate immediately and distinctly to the viewer or listener that your position has been distorted. Never overlook the hostile provocation of a Paraphraser. Be alert for it, and deal with it firmly.

The Dart Thrower

The most dangerous type of hostile interviewer is probably the Dart Thrower. Negative, antagonistic implications are buried in questions posed by this individual. He or she tries to convict you, your company or organization and all your colleagues by innuendo: "You know, I've watched you greedy, insensitive business tycoons coming to the public time after time to explain your intenuous position . . ." Then comes the question.

Your interviewer has just characterized you, your company or organization and your colleagues as greedy and insensitive with an untenable position. If you don't respond to that hostile characterization, you are tacitly acknowledging it could be true. Never answer a Dart Thrower's question without *first* addressing yourself to the innuendo.

Don't let any antagonistic innuendo go unanswered. Instead, respond directly to the hostile statement. "Just a minute, Susan. Before I answer your question, I must object to the form in which you addressed it. We in the XYZ Company are far from greedy or insensitive. We care about this community and all the people in it. That's why we . . ." and then go on to list all the programs your company or organization has undertaken to benefit your local schools, beautify the neighborhood, sponsor cultural events or otherwise show concern for the public.

Then, and only then, go on and answer the question asked.

Hostile Opponents

On occasion, a broadcast interview will cast you in the role of a debater, representing one side of an issue, usually controversial, that involves your company or your industry.

In most such situations, an informative discussion will ensue. Having done your homework and prepared thoroughly for the encounter, you will enjoy the challenge.

It doesn't always work that way, though. Sometimes, your opponent will take on the characteristics of a Machine Gun, an Interrupter, a Paraphraser or a Dart Thrower, and will use the very same hostile tactics.

Deal with that opponent just as you would a hostile interviewer. Use the proven techniques that allow you to keep the initiative, to stay in control.

If your opponent attacks you during the broadcast with an emotional, overwrought indictment of you, your company or your industry, a simple pause can be an efficient way to regain control of the pace of the interview. Take a long, deep breath. Pause. Let the hysteria of your opponent's remarks become almost visible to the viewer or listener. Then make a very quiet, measured response. The contrast will be evident to all.

If you're in a broadcast debate with a hostile opponent, seize the initiative by asking some questions of your own:

"What's the source of your information?" "Where did you *get* that idea?" Putting your opponent on the defensive can be an effective way to make a point and reassert control.

Another way to deflect a hostile opponent is to seek out areas of common ground and agreement. Do a little advance research. If your opponent has written a book critical of your industry or published an article that crucifies your profession, study that book or article and seek out every possible viewpoint with which you agree. In the interview, concentrate on those areas. Point out every topic on which you and your opponent are not in conflict. That way, you'll deflect your opponent's arguments and deflate his or her hostility. Instead of a knock-down, drag out fight, your confrontation will be a mild-mannered discussion, with you in the driver's seat.

And don't waste your air time by restating the views of your opponents. They get enough air time of their own. Don't repeat the accusation of an opponent. "I know people say we're insensitive, but we're not." Instead, use the time to state your own position: "I'll let my opponents speak for themselves. I can only speak for my own company, and *we* believe . . ."

Keep Your Cool

The goal of a hostile interviewer, or an antagonistic opponent, is not to get a good story or to make a point. It's to get you emotionally involved, and to make you lose control and credibility.

If you succumb to their tactics, you'll be goaded into making statements you'll later regret. And just as quickly, you'll lose your credibility with the viewer or listener.

So stay detached and unemotional. Maintain a polite, distant, measured stance. Close out all distractions and concentrate totally on dealing with the adversary. Keep cool.

You can and will succeed in converting a potentially damaging broadcast interview into an effective communications opportunity for yourself and your company or organization.

chapter ten

Dealing with Broadcasters in a Crisis Situation

No matter how valuable or necessary your product, or how reasonable or essential your service, your organization will not succeed for long if it does not enjoy a good reputation among customers, clients, opinion leaders, peers, stockholders, regulatory agencies, civic groups, employees and the people of your community.

Public confidence and good will are critical to the success of every business and nonprofit organization. Under ordinary circumstances, good will is a natural by-product of a business or organization operated honestly and offering true value for its goods or services.

However, public confidence in your business or organization may sometimes be threatened by forces seemingly beyond your control. A strike, employee layoffs, an accident at your plant, a rumor, an arrest of a key employee, a lawsuit—any of these can catapult a tranquil business enterprise or nonprofit organization into a crisis situation and into the headlines.

When crisis strikes, radio and television, with their voracious appetites for news and information, will probably be the first on the scene. Crisis means drama. Broadcast thrives on drama.

So you can almost count on it. Whether you want them or not, the cameras and microphones will be there. Ask the makers of Tylenol, the utility executives at Three Mile Island or the spokesperson of any chemical company accused of producing a carcinogen. Whether or not there's been a new development, the news of your crisis will be repeated over and over on air throughout the day—on morning drive time radio, the noon news, afternoon drive time, early evening newscasts and late night updates. Broadcasters with deadlines that may not be convenient for you will want comments at all hours of the day and night, but if you schedule an afternoon news conference to tell your side of the story, those same broadcasters will probably edit your twenty-minute presentation into a twenty-second sound bite, or maybe they won't show up at all.

Inconvenient! Infuriating! Inconsistent! Inevitable! Broadcast news is here to stay. It's getting more competitive, yet it's trusted and heeded by more Americans every day.

Dealing with the broadcast media in a crisis does have its positive side though, and it's a significant one to remember. "Balanced coverage," or presentation of contrasting views on "issues of public importance," is required of broadcasters under the FCC Fairness Doctrine. (See Chapter One.) That means you can nearly always expect to get your turn at bat in broadcast coverage of your crisis. With some effort, and some insight into the special requirements of radio and television journalism, you can make that turn at bat an effective avenue of communication with the public.

Here are some guidelines to help you deal with the broadcast media in periods of crisis.

THE BEST DEFENSE IS A STRONG OFFENSE

There is no substitute for the relationship of mutual respect developed with broadcasters in your day-to-day operations, *before* any crisis erupts. That's why so much of this book is devoted to practical suggestions for building effective communications bridges between your company or organization and the radio and television media in your community.

So be sure there is someone in your company or organization who has cordial, up-to-date contacts with someone at each and every radio and television station in your community. Don't forget the local cable system. (See Chapter Three for guidelines in building these essential professional contacts.) The person responsible for building and maintaining those media relationships needs to be clearly connected with the decision making process of top level management, and tuned in to the inner workings of your company or organization.

A strong working relationship with the broadcast media is tremendously helpful to your company or organization in its routine operations. In a period of crisis, it is invaluable.

Be Available When the News Is Bad

It's one thing to be available to broadcasters to talk about the benefits of your new product, or to describe how your organization is serving the senior citizens or youth or underprivileged of your community. But where are you when the news is bad?

> The head of a lobbying group promoting nuclear energy appeared on a nationally televised talk show to argue for the safety and reliability of nuclear power plants. The segment was quite successful, and the lobbyist followed up with a note to the talk show host, inviting him to tour what he termed "the safest nuclear facility ever built." The letter and invitation arrived just a few days before that very same facility hit the headlines with a "disaster story." The broadcaster did his best to contact the lobbyist and accept his invitation to tour the facility with network cameras. When his phone calls were never returned, he told his millions of viewers about the episode by reading the fateful letter on air.

Your relationship with broadcast journalists shouldn't be all one-sided. There are times when those journalists need *you*— to offer some insight on an issue that affects your industry, to help balance a news report on a controversial subject, to answer questions raised by your critics.

Your reluctance to come forward and volunteer information in such situations is understandable. But it may also be shortsighted. If you can be helpful to the broadcaster when he or she needs your participation, and if you are willing to make an effort even when it's not particularly beneficial to you, you will be making an important investment in building that bridge of trust and good will between yourself and the broadcast media.

> A local television news team was investigating allegations of "redlining" against the banking industry in the community. Critics charged that financial institutions were quietly refusing to make investments or mortage loans in areas heavily populated by minorities. But reporters were having difficulty producing a balanced report because, despite all their efforts, executives of almost every bank they contacted declined to talk on camera about the issue.
>
> But one bank came forward. A credible spokesperson was provided to discuss the issue candidly. The report was aired and the bank was fairly represented. That's not the end of this story. For years to come, the newscasters of that television station turned to the cooperative bank whenever they needed comment on a financial story. Again and again that bank's spokespersons were invited to talk about interest rates, IRA's, all-savers, money market funds—gaining thousands of dollars worth of visibility, solid publicity and good will—and probably many new customers for the institution.

Putting your company or organization in the spotlight when the news is adverse can involve some risk. But that risk will more often than not pay off in a better long-term relationship between your company or organization, the broadcast media and, ultimately, the public who look to radio and television for news and information.

Conversely, refusing to cooperate permits speculation, rumor, and conjecture to replace truth and facts.

Include Broadcasters in Your Crisis Planning

You can't plan a crisis, but you *can* plan how your company or organization will respond to the unexpected. The complexity of your crisis planning depends on the size of your company or organization and the kinds of emergencies you must be prepared to face. But whatever your size or your potential for controversy, it is essential to give some thought to how you will respond in the event of a crisis or catastrophe. Most enlightened businesses and nonprofit organizations today have, or are developing, carefully considered crisis plans. These plans usually cover how the business or organization will deal with all the various interest groups affected in the event of a crisis situation—employees, people of the community, and especially, the news media.

But no crisis plan is complete today unless it includes attention to the special needs and demands of the broadcast media. Dealing with a broadcast journalists is different from dealing with print reporters. Make sure your crisis plan is sensitive to the unique requirements of radio and television reporters. This may be as simple as providing soft drinks or hot coffee for waiting camera crews at your plant door. It may mean special electronic equipment—microphone banks, telephones, electrical outlets—in areas where radio, and particularly television news reporters will be working during the emergency period. It may be a willingness on your part to provide home phone numbers for key spokespersons so they can be contacted during off-hours, because broadcast news reports often need continuous updating round-the-clock. It may mean making sure your written news releases and bulletins are concise and distilled enough to fit the condensed time frame of the broadcast media.

Keep Broadcasters Informed

There will be times when you can see a crisis looming before it erupts. When negotiations are breaking down in contract talks with your employee union, you can be prepared for a possible work slowdown or even a strike. When both sides have offered the final arguments in a controversial court case involving your organization, you ought to know how you'll respond if the decision is negative.

When you're aware of a coming crisis, and you know it will produce headlines in your community, you may want to plan a carefully orchestrated backgrounder session for local print reporters and broadcasters. This offers you the opportunity to take the initiative, to encourage reporters, especially broadcasters, to cover the issue in a fair and balanced manner, and to provide them with the perspective and the information they need to do so.

Consider Visual Perceptions

Television is a visual medium. Television reporters need more than words to tell their stories—they need pictures. It may be tempting to decide unequivocally that you will not allow the television cameras at the scene of your disaster, and there may be times when that's the only possible decision you can make.

But don't decide to exclude television cameras without carefully considering the alternative. Remember, if your crisis is believed to be an important story by the station's news editors, it will be covered on television anyway. And there will be pictures accompanying that story anyway. If they aren't taken with your permission and your involvement, then they'll be taken independently—perhaps pictures of your closed door, or of employees picketing outside your gate, or of demonstrators chanting slogans, or an aerial view of the problem area shot from a helicopter.

Viewers of television news are affected as much by what is seen as by what is said. Consider the visual impact on viewers when you decide how to work with television reporters at the scene of a crisis. Think visually, and try to provide a setting that will support and enhance with visuals the position you are taking in words.

> A major manufacturer was being sued by an employee who charged "reverse discrimination" because he had not received an anticipated promotion. Although sympathetic, the company's position was that its decision adhered to the affirmative action laws of the land. The firm agreed to a network request for an interview with its labor relations expert.
>
> The executive's office was an imposing wood-paneled suite with an impressive view of the city below. But the televised interview wasn't held in that sumptuous setting in the corporate tower. Instead, the company arranged for its spokesperson

to be interviewed out-of-doors, at the gate of the plant, in shirt sleeves. The result was an interview that made that executive appear approachable and human rather than isolated and superior. When he told the interviewer how concerned the company was about the rights of every employee, his words were believably reinforced by the pictures.

Choose One Qualified Spokesperson

In any crisis, the broadcast media needs responses from your company or organization that are both accurate and consistent. Updates are often required quickly for frequent and fixed deadlines. To meet that need, and to avoid confusion and chaos, decide on one single spokesperson to speak for you in a period of crisis.

The individual you choose should be articulate and able to communicate complex ideas clearly. He or she should be cool under pressure and be plugged into top level management decisions during the crisis period. He or she should know and understand the media, and have the respect of the broadcast journalists. Sometimes, that credibility is best found at top level of management:

> A story broke on the newswire about a leakage at a small chemical plant located in a rural area. Allegedly, the leak was causing brown spots on lettuce crops of farms in the area.
>
> Network television crews were sent to the plant to take pictures and interview the plant manager for the newscast that evening. The manager hadn't seen the wire story allegations and was ill prepared for the news professionals who suddenly appeared at his doorstep.
>
> He panicked, barred the door and refused to talk on camera. The company president was alerted and took quick action. He phoned all the networks. "Use your pictures and I'll do your interview," he said. "I'll be at your studio before your deadline to answer all your questions and explain the company's position." He appeared as promised, and the company got a fair shake on the network reports. The crisis was defused.

Don't leave your employees in the trenches, ill prepared to handle a potentially damaging situation. When crisis strikes, identify the person who knows the issue best, and who has the authority and credibility to represent your company or organization on air. If you are that person, accept the responsibility. It will be well worth the energy and time you invest.

Take the Initiative

The president of that chemical plant did more than rescue his plant manager from an unpleasant experience or a damaging situation. He took the initiative. He provided more complete information than the broadcasters could have obtained on their own. He brought information to them, quickly enough to meet their deadlines, in a form suitable for broadcast.

In a crisis situation, you have two choices. You can sit back passively and wait for the bad news to hit air, and then react. Or, you can act. Take the initiative. Volunteer information. Tell reporters what happened, why it happened, and most importantly, what you are doing to correct the problem.

WHEN THE MEDIA CALL

There are occasions when a crisis explodes without warning. You're enjoying a predinner cocktail with your wife or husband when the phone rings. It's the business correspondent from the network affiliate thirty miles from your plant, asking about the million dollar antitrust suit your competitor just filed against you.

Don't Respond Off the Cuff

If you first inkling of a problem erupting in your company or organization comes from a journalist's call, it's hardly ever a good idea to respond off the top of your head. Being available doesn't mean being casual or careless.

Better to thank the caller for the information, ask what his or her deadline is, explain why you can't respond immediately, and promise to call back with the requested information. Then get the facts, verify them, and make some necessary decisions about how to proceed from that point. You owe it to yourself and your company or organization to make sure you're fully informed and throughly prepared before making that first critical statement.

Increasingly, business and nonprofit organizations are staging crisis seminars, either with outside counsel or with skilled internal personnel, to prepare executives to deal with the "worst case" scenario. These seminars help top level spokespersons anticipate probing or hostile questions and respond to them honestly and effectively. (For guidelines on broadcast interview techniques, see Chapter Nine.)

> Reporters got wind of rumors of seepage at a toxic waste disposal site, late one afternoon, at about the same time the company officials at the manufacturing plant did. The company scheduled a news conference for early the next morning. Company officials spent a grueling night anticipating all possible questions and preparing responses. The news conference was packed with journalists. The company position was made clear and its program for resolving the problem was emphasized in all subsequent news reports. The crisis was averted.

You won't always have the luxury of waiting until the following day to respond to a crisis situation. But take the time you need to decide on your best response and when appropriate, discuss the situation with your legal counsel. Your attorney's guidance may prevent you from saying in haste something you may later regret.

Consider Advantages of One-on-One Media Contacts

A news conference like the one just described can be a valuable way to quickly defuse a crisis. But sometimes dealing with the media in a group situation, especially the highly competitive broadcast media, can be fraught with peril. In the news conference setting, you run the risk of letting one hostile reporter set the tone, of having the media "gang up" on you, and of losing control of the situation.

Don't plan a news conference when the details of your crisis or catastrophe are still unfolding, when you aren't sure you know all the details, or when you're not absolutely confident you can wrap the whole controversy up in one upfront session with the media.

Instead, it's usually preferable to deal with the news reporters one-on-one. That way you can personalize your message to meet the concerns of each reporter or interviewer without playing favorites. It is time consuming and tedious, but the payoff will probably be better, tolerant, more fair and even-handed coverage of your side of the story.

When you *do* decide a news conference is the best way to go, make sure to go into it thoroughly prepared. Do a mock interview, draw up a list of every possible hostile or embarrassing question that might surface, and decide how you'll answer each one. (See Chapter Nine.) Have four or five people from your public affairs department or some colleagues who are well-versed on the details of the crisis sit and grill you until you're certain you can handle any possible query.

In a crisis when emotions are often running high, it's critical to carefully plan your responses, especially when you face potentially negative questions. A period of crisis is the time for even more emphasis on clarity and believability. It's more important than ever that *you,* not the reporters, maintain control of media interviews.

Following are some guidelines to help you develop responses that clearly and effectively communicate your viewpoint.

• *Perspective.* When a sudden crisis strikes, we sometimes get so busy stamping out the fire we forget that the problem at hand developed as part of a whole historical context. We're so focused on the here and now we overlook the significance of walking back through the entire spectrum of events that led to the present situation.

Put the crisis in perspective. Talk about the many years your company has been in business, the contributions your firm has made to the local and national economy, the important products you've developed or services you've offered over the years. The current problem will not seem so overwhelming when you put it in that larger frame.

• *Clarifying Terms.* If a product you produce is labelled "carcinogenic," or your company is accused of dumping "toxic waste," you have a responsibility to clarify those terms. Don't passively accept labels that may trigger panic or fear in the public mind. "Toxic" is not synonymous with "deadly." "Carcinogenic" means "cancer-causing," not "lethal" or "fatal." The burden is on you to clarify terms, to be specific, to define meanings precisely. What kind of cancer? Who was exposed? What are the effects?

• *Positioning.* When a crisis occurs, it's important to carefully consider where your company or organization fits in the context of the issue at hand, then to articulate that position. The classic example of effective positioning was the major drug company whose product was tampered with, causing widespread panic and even death. From the beginning, the company saw clearly that it was not a perpetrator of this situation, but a victim, as much so as any individual harmed by the tampering. The consistent message, "We are victims too," was successful in winning sympathy and support from public and press.

• *Don't look back.* Once a situation has occurred or a decision has been made, often little can be done to change it. Don't let interviews become a rehash of past problems and past grievances. Look ahead, not back. Use the words of an executive of a chemical company facing allegations that a product manufactured at its plant a decade ago had caused occurrences of cancer among former workers. "What's done is done, and cannot be changed," the executive said. "Let me tell you what we are doing about the problem today." He continued by describing the programs the firm had put in place for locating, testing, and treating all former employees who had been exposed to the chemical substance.

Be Candid and Consistent; Speak With One Voice

Your response in a period of crisis must be as forthright and upfront as it can possibly be. Above all, you want your statements and your responses to be believed.

Consistency is paramount in dealing with any reporter in a crisis situation. Develop one theme or story line, then stick with it. Changing horses in midstream, changing your story, and issuing conflicting statements detracts from your credibility.

The immediacy of the broadcast media underscores the importance of consistency in your dealings with radio and television reporters. The broadcast journalist can—and often will—juxtapose two conflicting statements in the same report, and the resulting impact on the viewer can destroy your company or organization's credibility for years to come.

Don't Stonewall

The days of the "no comment" evasion are over. Ask ex-President Nixon and his colleagues. The media respond to openness and candor. When a reporter gets an impression that you're ducking the issue, he or she will go for the jugular.

Avoid at all costs any implication that you are stonewalling the press, ducking issues, or sweeping controversy under the rug. Don't blame your mistakes on someone else, or, worse yet, pretend they never happened.

> The executive of a major automobile manufacturer was interviewed on a television network news program after it had been revealed that the company had routinely been equipping one of its top-of-the-line cars with engines from a less expensive model. The executive never acknowledged that a mistake had been made. Instead, he ducked questions, and evaded the issue. But every time he gave an evasive answer, the panel of reporters pressed him with more questions. The interview lacked any credibility. This high level executive's evasive responses to an important public concern may have damaged the credibility of that manufacturer and the entire American automobile industry for years to come.

If this executive had anticipated the hostile questions and discussed possible responses with legal advisors, he surely could have planned some responsible, sincere answers that would have satisfied both his questioners and his corporation. A response like, "Yes, something went amiss here, and I can assure you and your viewers that as long as I am head of this company, it will never happen again," could have defused the antagonistic questions and changed the direction of the interview.

In some instances (provided you have the go-ahead from your legal counsel), an open admission of error, or an expression of compassion and caring is the best response you can make. If a mistake was made, and if your company or organization is in the wrong, say so. An apology is effective when it is delivered candidly and with sincerity.

> An executive of a leading chemical company was interviewed on television after the public had learned that the firm's manufacturing process had been blamed for the development of lung disease among some workers.
>
> The executive didn't vacillate or make excuses. Instead. he admitted the problem was "one of the bleakest chapters in our company's history." He said the plant would be closed permanently.
>
> The televised interview was effective because his admission of wrongdoing coupled with his compassion and concern for his employees was evident, both in his words and in the action the company was to take.

People will nearly always forgive a mistake if it's admitted openly, followed by a sincere apology, and if there is obvious sympathy for those who are affected adversely. People forgive because they make mistakes too.

Assert Your Rights

Just because your company or organization has found itself in a difficult situation, you need not take a passive or defensive posture. You can and should set some ground rules before submitting to broadcast interviews.

It's a mistake to assume that broadcast journalists are "out to get you" when your company or organization is involved in a crisis or emergency. Most journalists are just as concerned as you are about getting an accurate story and reporting it fairly.

> The chief executive of a major retail chain was interviewed on-location as he told why the company had decided to close its largest retail outlet located in an aging metropolitan area. It was a very sensitive decision, since the firm depended on sales to low-income families for a good percentage of its success. He was a little nervous as the cameras rolled, and he stammered a bit in his repsonses.
>
> Disappointed that he had represented the company position so poorly, this executive might have dismissed the poor interview as "one of those things." But he didn't. Instead, he asked the reporter for another chance to explain the decision. The cameras were brought back, the executive started again, and the result was a better, more effective interview.

If you remain cool and use good judgment, you may be surprised by how cooperative most broadcasters will be in helping to make certain your point of view is fairly represented.

Don't Overreact

You may not always be pleased with the way your side of the story is presented on radio or television. Sometimes, you may have a justifiable complaint about how equitably or accurately broadcasters aired the sensitive news about your problem.

But even when you're right, it's not always in your best interest to take action. Make sure some useful purpose is served when and if you decide to complain about how your story was covered.

> A major manufacturer was cited by a federal agency for allegedly claiming falsely that a product had fire-retardant qualities. The story hit network news, accompanied by a visual showing one of the company's ads. Unfortunately, the ad was not for the product being cited. Company executives were annoyed at the erroneous coverage. They demanded, and got, a public apology from the network. The apology may have been justified, but its positive effect on the company's image is questionable. It served as an opportunity for the network news

to highlight the same issue again. Thus it was a reminder to viewers who had seen the story the first time, and informed thousands more who had missed the initial newscast of that company's alleged wrongdoing.

Even when you think a correction of a broadcast story is justified, consider the side effects before insisting on that correction. What will it gain to win the battle? What purpose will it serve?

There are other situations in which the broadcaster's error seems more deliberate, more hostile. A hostile situation can sometimes develop rapidly between a broadcaster and a company or organization involved in a crisis. And in the competitive arena of broadcast news reporting, there may be some journalists who overstep the bounds of ethics in their efforts to be first with the story.

In those situations, the naturally adversarial relationship between you and the broadcaster can quickly deteriorate into one of confrontation and hostility.

> A network newsman went unannounced to a Fortune 500 company's strip mining site and proceeded to film the operation. Security people at the mine saw him, confiscated his camera, and detained him for several hours.
>
> The reporter was wrong. But the company overreacted. When the news report on strip mining finally aired, it was a scathing indictment of that company and its practices.

Even when you are right and the broadcast journalist is wrong, don't come on too strong. Don't overreact. Don't strain that adversarial relationship more than is absolutely necessary to protect your interests. Keep cool and remember the journalist is under pressure, too. Antagonizing the media unnecessarily is a mistake that may haunt you long after today's crisis is a dim memory.

Protect Yourself

If you foresee special problems in your dealings with the broadcast media, there are precautions you can take to help protect your company or organization from biased or hostile reporting.

More and more companies and organizations are keeping their own independent records of broadcast interviews. These audiotapes, videotapes, and transcripts are helpful in the event a question arises later about what actually was said.

Others are developing in-house training programs or hiring consultants to teach top level management how to deal with the broadcast media effectively.

GET IN THE RING

Crisis reporting almost always means bad news. And most of us want to keep our company or organization as distant from bad news as we can.

Though it's tempting to shy away from getting involved in the unfavorable news that's almost inevitably the result of a crisis situation, don't give in to that temptation. Almost always, the worst thing you can do in any crisis situation is to do nothing.

Refusing to comment, pleading confidentiality, or failing to return the phone calls of reporters will harm your company or organization as much or more than the most damaging news report. And the harm won't just be for today—for months, years or even permanently, it could break down that long-term trust and mutual respect you want to build with the broadcast media.

Getting into the ring can be risky. You may get a black eye or a bloody nose, but you will have had your say. Chances are good that you will emerge from the encounter with renewed respect from the media and from the public whose goodwill you want and need to conduct your business or provide your service successfully.

Summing Up

"For all who want to take part in the continuing telecommunications adventure, it's time to get ready for the future."

This challenge to communicators wasn't sounded just last week or last month. It's from the pages of a September, 1980 issue of *Broadcasting Magazine.*

It is a challenge that business and industry leaders and the public relations professionals who work with them must take to heart. It is a challenge this book was written to help you meet.

In this age of electronic communications, the future of public relations is intertwined with broadcast. That means radio. That means television. That means cable systems and all the other advances of the emerging new communications technologies.

If you're in business, industry or a nonprofit organization with a story to tell and you're still working exclusively with the print media, you're not in tune with today, and you're certainly not in touch with tomorrow. To get ready for the future, you need to understand both the *why* and the *how* of broadcast public relations. That's what this book set out to accomplish.

Why broadcast public relations? Because of the amazing growth in the power, reach, and influence of the electronic media. Because of the everexpanding array of attractive opportunities for getting your story to the public. Because it works.

How to accomplish effective broadcast public relations? If you're a public relations professional, by acquiring a working acquaintance with the broadcasters of your community. By learning to present your ideas to a broadcaster in writing and to format your message to "play" well on radio or television.

If you're the business executive or organization leader who will speak for your company or group, by developing the attitudes and techniques you need to convey your message convincingly and forthrightly under the pressure of the live microphone or the studio lights; and by updating your crisis planning to meet the needs of radio and television journalists as well as print reporters.

These are the how-to's, the techniques of broadcast public relations. They are the skills and attitudes you need to participate in that continuing adventure of broadcast communications. And what's more, as was stressed throughout this book, once you master those techniques and skills, you will be able to communicate effectively through the broadcast media despite any technological innovations, or any "gee-whiz" developments on the telecommunications scene.

As we've repeated again and again, the delivery systems are changing and doubtless will continue to change. But the techniques we've talked about today will still be relevant for you tomorrow.

Business, industry, and nonprofit organizations have a story to tell. The public relations professionals are the storytellers.

Learn to tell your story on radio and television today, and you will be part of the media mix for many years to come.

FOOTNOTES

Chapter One

1. Arthur M. Schlesinger Jr., *The Coming of the New Deal* (Boston, MA: Houghton Mifflin Co., 1958), pp. 571–572.

2. John Crosby, "It Was New and We Were Innocent," *TV Guide —The First 25 Years,* compiled by Jay S. Harris (New York, NY: Simon and Schuster, 1978), p. 211.

3. Dwight Whitney, "America's Long Vigil," *TV Guide—The First 25 Years,* compiled by Jay S. Harris (New York, NY: Simon and Schuster, 1978), p. 82.

4. NASA Public Affairs Newsroom. Media Services Unit, Mary Fitzpatrick.

5. James Mann, "What Is TV Doing to America?" *US News and World Report,* August 22, 1982, pp. 27–30.

6. Robert MacNeil, *The Right Place at the Right Time* (New York, NY: Little, Brown and Company, 1982), p. 301.

7. AV Westin, *Newswatch* (New York, NY: Simon and Schuster, 1982), p. 56. Reprinted by permission of the publisher.

8. *Radio Facts,* Radio Advertising Bureau. New York, NY, 1981.

9. Television Bureau of Advertising, New York, NY, 1981.

FIGURE 1.

MICHAEL KLEPPER ASSOCIATES
Interview Schedule

Guest's Name _____

Client _____

Tour City _____

Tour Date _____

This Schedule As Of _____

Copies To _____

Scheduled By _____

TIME	STATION/PUBLICATION	AIR DATE/TIME	RATINGS/CIRC.	COMMENTS
Arrival Time: Interview Time: Live/Taped	 Phone:			Contact: Format: Topic: NB:
Arrival Time: Interview Time: Live/Taped	 Phone:			Contact: Format: Topic: NB:
Arrival Time: Interview Time: Live/Taped	 Phone:			Contact: Format: Topic: NB:

Index